INTELLIGENT CURIOSITY

The Art of Finding More

To Kevin Gillies,

Jim Cathcart

WRITTEN BY

JIM CATHCART

Author of *The Acorn Principle* and *The Power Minute*

WITH

LISA PATRICK

INTELLIGENT **CURIOSITY**

Quantity sales special discounts are available on quantity purchases by corporations, associations, and others. For details, contact the publisher at the address above.

Orders by U.S. and Canada trade bookstores and wholesalers. Email info@ BeyondPublishing.net

The Beyond Publishing Speakers Bureau can bring authors to your live event. For more information or to book an event contact the Beyond Publishing Speakers Bureau speak@BeyondPublishing.net

The Author can be reached directly at Cathcart.com and LisaPatrick.ca

Manufactured and printed in the United States of America distributed globally by BeyondPublishing.net

BEYOND
PUBLISHING

New York | Los Angeles | London | Sydney

ISBN Hardcover: 978-1-637921-24-1

ISBN Softcover: 978-1-637921-23-4

ENDORSEMENTS

The only way to gain new knowledge is through opening your mind and seeing things through different lenses. As humans, we are innately curious but we tend to tamper that curiosity, accepting a certain level of mediocrity. Those who remain curious and are intelligent about what they can still do, learn and become, enjoy more success and more satisfaction with their lives. Kudos to Jim Cathcart and Lisa Patrick for helping us all re-discover our curiosity through the concepts in this book. - **Tom Hopkins, CPAE | Author of How to Master the Art of Selling and When Buyers Say No**

Jim Cathcart and Lisa Patrick have always impressed me with their honesty and professionalism. Both are gifted speakers and writers and now co-authors of a new book, Intelligent Curiosity. It's the art of finding more. Isn't that our quest in life to find more and live our short life with passion and curiosity? This book is for you! Buy it, read it and apply its principles to your life, to find that magic spot for you. - **Dr. Peter Legge, OBC, LL.D (Hon) D. Tech. CSP, CPAE | Chairman Canada Wide Media Ltd.**

I'm curious about why this wonderful book hasn't been written sooner! As children, we are always asking... "Why?" As we age, that seems to happen less and less. This book, written by my former partner and dear friend Jim Cathcart and my colleague Lisa Patrick, helps us rekindle that childhood curiosity. In fact, it elevates your existing amount of curiosity to a level of "Intelligent Curiosity" which is directed, focused, strategic and intentional. Invest in this book and develop this Edge Learning skill of Intelligent Curiosity that can readily be developed to your benefit." - **Dr. Tony Alessandra, Author of The Platinum Rule® and Charisma | Chairman Assessments24x7**

Lisa Patrick and Jim Cathcart's Intelligent Curiosity – The Art Of Finding More is packed with stimulating ideas that cause even the most ambitious of us to ponder. They encourage us to take advantage of challenging times to revisit, refocus, and re-energize with our God-given curiosity.- **Patricia Fripp, CSP, CPAE, Hall of Fame, Past President, National Speakers Association - FRIPPVT.com**

Jim Cathcart and his innovative concept of Intelligent Curiosity brings a new, inspiring view of how to see the world and create new opportunities that unlock your potential. Thanks, Jim and Lisa, for writing such a fascinating book! - **Jason Dorsey, bestselling author of Zconomy: How Gen Z Will Change the Future of Business and What To Do About It**

Lisa will impart piercing wisdom to you while uplifting your world and making you feel a sense of purpose, value, and deep relationship. From the moment I met Lisa, I knew that her energy and creativity would positively impact my life and everyone she has touched. Understanding the skill of Intelligent Curiosity of Edge Learning is a must! You will want to read this book! - **Patrick Sells, Head of Bank Solutions NYDIG, 2020 American Banker's "Digital Banker of the Year"**

Lisa has an extremely unique gift of simplifying complex concepts so that they can be easily understood, but even more importantly, easily implemented. Her desire to help people access their potential is unmatched and I am excited to witness the millions of breakthroughs that will transpire because of this book.- **Jared Yellin, Co-Founder of 10X Incubator | A Grant Cardone Company**

Startups succeed when the founders innovate while continually seeking feedback and validation for their ideas. This coupled with the drive and determination to make smart decisions creates a pathway to success. This book will teach the skills required to be "Intelligently Curious. A must read and re-read. - **Alec Stern, 8-time Co-Founder; including Constant Contact | Founding Team Member | "America's Startup Success Expert" | AlecSpeaks.com**

One edge that introverts have is analytical reflection. This allows them the space to be what my friend and colleague Jim Cathcart calls "intelligently curious." In this wonderful book, you will learn how to carefully explore your ideas and opportunities, and gain the confidence to take bold action. A highly recommended read that will spur your entire team to success! - **Matthew Pollard, Best Selling Author of The Introvert's Edge Series**

Opportunities in life are not only created by those who are relentlessly curious and put themselves in the position of "Eligible Receiver," but also to those who have the desire and ability to catch them and get into the end zone. That is the fundamental difference between those who succeed vs. those who will spend their lives waiting and wondering when it will be their turn – as if greatness is a lottery vs. a deliberate and intentional effort. What Jim and Lisa are espousing in this book is that in order to be successful, however you define it, opportunities are created by those who realize life is not a spectator sport and are driven by Intelligent Curiosity. I have known Lisa for many years and she has always been someone I have had an opportunity to learn from. Every day is a school day when you are connected to Lisa and this book will inspire you towards Intelligent Curiosity... - **Duncan Bureau, Co-founder The LorEau Group, Co-Founder The LorEau Aviation Group, Owner Fit2Fly, Chief Commercial Officer Canada Jetlines, Dad to the world's most amazing kid, author, speaker and Klosebuy Board member.**

Innovation creates transformational game changers, and when you learn to deploy your inner curiosity to the problems you are dealing with, you can clearly see new solutions and possibilities. My long time friend and colleague Jim Cathcart and Lisa Patrick have now provided a skill book on Intelligent Curiosity. When you learn how to direct your curiosity and how to explore it, you can anticipate and innovate with confidence. **-Daniel Burrus, New York Times and Amazon bestselling author of seven books including his latest, The Anticipatory Organization**

Lisa and Jim have brilliantly taken up a topic and written extensively on child-like curiosity which is the fountain of many discoveries and inventions in the world. All the more these traits are important in today's world of information overload to find our own moorings being intelligently curious vis a vis herd mentality consensus information.

Lisa has ignited all old age vedic principles of questioning and being rational plus constantly evolving. Being curious ignites truthfulness which is the binding factor of the universe. **- Umesh Nair, Member Of The Board Of Advisors: Vipper.com, VoiceMe.AI, FASTsystemsAG**

"Success is all around us all of the time! We simply need to learn the principles and techniques in how to identify and capture it into our lives. In his latest masterpiece, Jim Cathcart, along with Lisa Patrick, teach you the amazing step-by-step process in bringing light onto your awareness in the book Intelligent Curiosity - The Art of Finding More. There is much more to life if you allow yourself the tools to truly be intelligently curious." **- Speaker Erik Swanson - 10 Time #1 Best Selling Author, Founder & CEO Habitude Warrior Mastermind**

DEDICATIONS

This book is dedicated to my adult grandchildren Jason Tyler Cathcart and Amber Marie Cathcart. They, along with their parents Jim Cathcart Jr. and Sonya, will carry the Cathcart legacy into the future. May you never stop asking, "Is that really so? Why? How do I know this assumption is valid? Have I explored enough sources to know I should rely on this one?"
All four of you make me immensely proud to be "Dad or Grandpa Jim." I am amazed at your brilliance and the beauty in your hearts.

———

This book is dedicated to my amazing daughters, Olivia and Jorga. May you always have the courage to find more and be curious in the pursuit of your dreams. I am so honoured to be your mom and proud of the young women you have become.

"I stood frozen looking through the pane glass window, waiting, afraid to breathe on the window for fear the person could see my breath fog the glass.

I'd spent the last two hours listening intently as the Detective asked intelligent questions of the 6 year-old little boy who was riddled in tears, with a goose egg the size of a golf ball on his forehead.

The police file I had been pouring over for the last week was 6 inches thick with one horrific story after another about this little boy and the abuse he had endured throughout his short life.

I was 21 years old and this was the first time I ever got to witness the detectives using their Edge Learning skills to help them conduct an interview. What I didn't know then was how important the Edge Learning skill of Intelligent Curiosity would become in my professional career."

Lisa Patrick

………………………….

When Jim Cathcart chose human development as his professional path he didn't even know what to wonder about. He'd seen charismatic speakers hold an audience spellbound but had no clue that this was a learnable craft. Jim just wanted to be around self-improvement and the kinds of people it attracted.

Jim had a simple goal. Become a trainer who helped others learn success skills. But he had not personally succeeded yet and had no education that would make him worthy of such a role. Professional Speakers, Private Investigators, Researchers, Philosophers, Authors and Business Owners were beyond his pay grade in so many ways.

He didn't know where to start. But he was curious and that was enough.

TABLE OF CONTENTS

INTRODUCTION

Curiosity didn't kill the cat, it created a mousetrap.

Mousetraps made house cats unnecessary for pest control. Still great pets, but no longer needed to eliminate mice. Somebody saw the problem and asked, "What is another way?"

Every living being is a problem solver. And problems are solved through curiosity. Every invention and innovation in the history of mankind began with curiosity. "Hmmm, I wonder how that works?"

We're all familiar with the old tale of the goose that lays the golden egg. We remember that the short-sighted farmer grew impatient and killed the goose to get all the golden eggs at once only to realize that subsequently, he'd get no more eggs, and the goose was just an ordinary goose. The moral of the story is that when you care more about the byproduct than asking intelligently curious questions about why and what is producing the results (the source) you'll end up destroying both.

Curiosity is defined as an emotion. Feeling curious is 100 percent natural to us as infants and toddlers. We are born curious and are highly-attuned to the world around us. We take in an inordinate amount of information during the first few years of life through curious experimentation. Sadly, few adults value that emotion or take advantage of its incredible power.

The noted Irish statesman and philosopher Edmund Burke is quoted as saying, "The first and simplest emotion which we discover in the human mind is curiosity." "First" and "simplest." If only he'd mentioned how extraordinary that emotion is!

The goal of this book is to help you convert your innate emotion of curiosity into a skill; one that will help you achieve greater success more rapidly than you imagined. We are not offering another "shiny object" or theory about how to succeed. What is presented in this book is an elevation of your existing emotion of curiosity to a level of "Intelligent Curiosity." Intelligent Curiosity is directed, focused, strategic and intentional. It is more than an emotion; it's a soft skill that can readily be developed to your benefit. It is like public speaking, a learnable skill. Anyone can speak, but to speak before a group and compel them to actually take action, that is a powerful skill.

Albert Einstein understood this concept well. When asked about his genius, he stated, *"I have no special talent. I am only passionately curious."*

We are hardwired to be curious. Think about every time you see something you don't immediately understand. For example, what happens when you drive by a motor vehicle accident? You become the rubbernecker. You're curious about what happened, how it happened and what the end result is for those involved. It's so natural to us to "want to know" that most give that emotion little thought. We certainly don't lack curiosity. We just don't think of it as being a skill that can be nurtured to our benefit.

Visionary, innovator and gifted conceptual thinker, Dan Sullivan, refers to curiosity as a "unique skill" in adults. When we are curious we are more likely to come up with creative solutions to problems, uncover new possibilities and create previously unrecognized opportunities.

Your authors have each forged paths to success through unconventional means. Turning points occurred in each of their lives around the concept they have now named "Intelligent Curiosity." These turning points led to one, a young government worker at a job that required little skill, with commensurate low pay, becoming a best-selling author of 20 books, an in-demand international public speaker and university professor who holds no university degree! The other began a career in law enforcement then moved into private investigation, learning how to hide in the shadows with nary a thought about public speaking and today is a sought-after speaker and thought leader in the arena of Edge Learning, working with today's top professionals helping them advance from ideation to market.

Through their life experiences, their Intelligent Curiosity had become activated. They recognized what was happening and leaned into that activation. By doing so, they created opportunities where none existed before. They gained a deep understanding of the problem-solving steps associated with exploring unfamiliar topics and learning something new. And, the best news for you is that they found each other to collaborate on this book--your entrance into the world of Intelligent Curiosity.

Curiosity Sparks Innovation

To come up with better solutions for the many complex problems the world is facing, curious people generate unique ideas. However, many ideas don't just come to us in a moment of time, but rather germinate over time. Intelligent Curiosity causes us to open dialogues and encourage acceptance. It helps us to find ways of helping others and gaining their trust.

Everyone is curious, but not everyone is intelligently curious. Intelligent Curiosity looks beneath the surface of circumstances or situations--seeing beyond the obvious. It causes us to sense a deeper meaning, to recognize emerging patterns, and intuit the bigger picture of what's going on around us. It allows us to see opportunities others miss. When others seem satisfied, the Intelligently Curious keep on asking new questions.

To See or Not To See

Each of us has the ability to see and hear without actually perceiving. This means that we can be looking right at something yet it still escapes our awareness. This is called an "intellectual blind spot." Everyone has them. They are conditioned into us over time, but we can learn to transcend or even eliminate them. When we do, we will see more with the same effort.

When we learn how to be present with our circumstances – to "see" and feel and sense them – they reveal themselves to us. We will understand more fully the essence of what is going on; we will sense what wants to happen in the big picture; and intuitively, we will be shown our next steps.

We have been conditioned to analyze and find quick fixes for situations. We see the task at hand and execute the steps to get it done. However, by enhancing our curiosity to where it serves us to an even deeper level, we see beyond the obvious to greater opportunities to connect with others, to generate new business and to achieve greater results.

It may sound corny, but it's true. When you find a way to activate your curiosity to serve a specific purpose that you have in mind, positive results happen!

This book is to guide you about how to activate your Edge Learning skill of Intelligent Curiosity. To be more aware, focused, directed, strategic and intentional. Once you do, you will see beyond the obvious. You will create more possibilities. You will have more and better opportunities.

"The American child is a highly intelligent human being - characteristically sensitive, humorous, open-minded, eager to learn, and has a strong sense of excitement, energy, and healthy curiosity about the world in which he lives. Lucky indeed is the grown-up who manages to carry these same characteristics into adult life. It usually makes for a happy and successful individual." - Walt Disney

CHAPTER 1

WHAT IS INTELLIGENT CURIOSITY?

"The essence of intelligence is the ability to make distinctions. The more you notice, the more you know. The more you know, the more options you have. The person with the most options usually prevails." - Jim Cathcart

Intelligent Curiosity is knowing what to wonder about and how to discover it.

Look around. What do you notice? In your surroundings? About the people closest to you? About interactions between others? Chances are right now that you are somewhat aware of everything from the traffic outside, the sound of the air conditioner, noises made by others in your house (including pets), the sounds of the house itself, the weather, the chair you're sitting in, the clothes you're wearing and the emotions you're feeling. Most of these things are not currently receiving your direct attention or you wouldn't be reading these words, but you *are* aware of them on some level.

If you heard screeching tires and crunching metal, not only would you be aware of the noise of traffic but you'd likely become curious about what happened. As a looky-loo or bystander you may give that noise enough attention to recognize what happened--a vehicle accident. You might come to a decision as to how serious it is. You may even feel some sympathy for those involved. That's a natural or normal level of curiosity and reaction to events. We all have it. But you wouldn't necessarily feel connected to it.

When searching for the answers to the questions that plague us--in life or in business--a common practice is to remain distant and objective. Objectivity is lauded as a good strategy when analyzing the many factors at play. But subjectivity has its value as well. Sometimes you can learn even more by immersing yourself into the situation. You subjectively could ask, "How can I help?"

Run Toward The Problem

Another bit of advice is to consider what everyone else is doing and do the opposite. Rather than considering situations objectively or even at arm's length, this would mean getting closer to them, digging deeper with questions and analyzing the answers to each. In the case of the vehicle accident, you might move beyond "what happened" to "why did that happen?" You'd start to ask questions.

Cause
- Was the driver at fault?
- Was there a flaw in the vehicle?
- Was there road damage like a pothole?
- Were the traffic signals functioning properly?
- What was the weather at the time?
- Was it light or dark out?
- Was vision impaired in either direction?
- Was there a major distraction nearby?

The answer to each of those questions would likely lead you deeper and deeper into analysis until you discovered either the foundational cause or a combination of factors that contributed to the end result. The topic missing above is, the effect of the accident.

Effect
- Was anyone hurt?
- Do they need immediate help?
- Were others affected?
- Whose property was damaged?
- Is anything being done to assist?
- Would I be making matters worse by getting involved?

The process of seeking those answers would take you deeper and deeper into that situation. Along the path of seeking answers, you would likely discover and discard many possibilities, getting closer and closer to the true answer each time. In our experience, getting closer to the situation at hand is usually the better option. It requires the use of what we have identified as "Intelligent Curiosity." Intelligent Curiosity is directed, focused, strategic and intentional.

Context and Implications
- Does anything seem out of place here?
- What is there about this scene that doesn't make sense yet?
- How many options are there for solving this problem?
- Should we call the police, fire department or hospital?
- If I do nothing, what will happen?

- Is there any continuing danger that needs to be eliminated?
- What needs to happen once the emergency is dealt with?
- Who is the best person to take each action?

We propose that getting closer to situations encourages you to actually broaden your perspectives on them, which allows you to remain open to a wider variety of possible solutions than objectivity grants.

Cause, Effect, Context, Implications.

Intelligent Curiosity isn't to be confused with the mainstream definition of curiosity. By viewing situations, and the world itself, with Intelligent Curiosity, you are able to see beyond what's openly visible to others. You are more aware of the details and able to envision scenarios and potential solutions that are invisible to others. You are able to create opportunities that did not previously exist, and you become an "eligible receiver" of those opportunities.

While as humans we are innately curious about the world around us and the situations we encounter, the depth of our curiosity tends to diminish as we mature. We become accustomed to our surroundings. We default to the easiest, most common solutions for situations that arise. We accept other people's conclusions as to what is so. Some of us even become jaded to the world around us and purposely choose to stop exploring it. We develop mundane habits. We follow "the norms" rather than seeking out ideas or solutions that might be more creative or more beneficial to us. The end result is that many of us live lives below our potential. We never achieve those lofty goals we once had. We lose enthusiasm as the opportunities related to them just don't materialize. The application of Intelligent Curiosity brings about an entirely different way of seeing our problems and the routes to our goals. It can change all of that for the better.

Intelligent Curiosity Seeks Truth

One of the most beneficial skills to develop is learning how to apply Intelligent Curiosity to everyday situations. It's one thing to be curious in a light way, as in having a passing interest in something. Intelligent Curiosity is quite another. It operates at a much higher and deeper level. It's not even a matter of just being more deeply curious about something. When applying Intelligent Curiosity, you're curious with a specific purpose in mind. Implementing this depth of curiosity can be likened to using the scientific method where a problem is identified, relevant data is gathered, a hypothesis is formulated from the data, and the hypothesis is empirically tested.

When Lisa asked how Intelligent Curiosity has played into his success, author Seth Godin replied, *"Well, I will tell you the secret of 7,500 blog posts and 20 books. It's a simple secret, and I'm happy to give it away. If I can't figure out how something in the world works, it's very hard for me to go to sleep. I know that electricity is not a magic trick; I can tell you how it works. I know that my refrigerator does not have elves in it, who keep the milk cold; I can tell you how it works. I don't have any satisfaction in just seeing something in the world. Some businesses succeed, someone gets elected, Eastman Kodak fails, whatever it is, if I can't come up with a thesis, a hypothesis, a theory about why that happened. And my best blog posts are simply my explanation of something I saw in the world, and how I think it might work. And then if I can refine it, that's even better. So some people call that curiosity.*

And for me, it's part of my practice. Do not accept anything as a given without understanding how it fits into the system of our world."

Be forewarned when following the path of Intelligent Curiosity you may occasionally fall down a few rabbit holes. However, the information gleaned there may be necessary to help you discover what *isn't* the best answer to something.

Intelligent Curiosity is a learnable skill. It requires commitment to stay highly focused and to allow a longer time frame to discover the best answers to your questions. In a society that wants fast, short answers to everything, Intelligent Curiosity goes against the norm. You may end up with the same solution as someone who chooses to get answers within three clicks on Google. However, when you come up with an entirely different solution, you'll be convinced of its validity because of your diligence. While others may find the right answer by luck, you will have found it by intelligent analysis. You can say, "This works, and I know why it works." And, best of all, you'll avoid the pitfall of confirmation bias.

Confirmation bias is when you seek out answers to prove your instincts right.

It doesn't necessarily mean you've discovered the best answer. It just means you've found the answer you thought was true. That's when most people stop exploring. Answer found, problem solved, Next! We all want to be right. The challenge comes when we assume being "right" also means being "best."

When we desire an idea or concept to be true, we will only seek evidence to make it so. Once confirmed, we stop further inquiry. We don't look beyond the "evidence" or even allow for the potential of a better solution. The application of Intelligent Curiosity keeps us from becoming prisoners of our own assumptions. It helps us to become aware of our psychological blind spots.

Here's an example of confirmation bias: Imagine that you are trying to reach a friend. When you last spoke, you said something that you now consider might have been in bad taste and you want to clarify your meaning. You send a text: "Hey, are you available for a quick call?" No response. You call and it goes to voicemail. You may try a direct message through social media as well. Again, there's no immediate reply. You start to wonder if your friend is upset with you. Are they trying to distance themself from you? You may start to think you just need to give them some time. The danger of accepting the belief that they are upset with you without questioning it further may prevent you from exploring other possibilities. Instead, you will begin to behave toward this friend under the assumption that the story you've created in your mind is true. Confirmation bias is telling you that you're right. You are only considering the information that confirms your thinking, expectations or suspicions.

Utilizing Intelligent Curiosity in this situation will help you think of what else might be happening. Perhaps your friend is sleeping. Maybe their phone needs charging. Perhaps they are somewhere they can't have their phone on or where there's little-to-no service. Maybe they went out and forgot to take their phone. Maybe your friend is helping someone else through a crisis and is choosing not to check their phone. Rather than allowing confirmation bias to cause you to settle on the self-serving answer that it's all about you, employ Intelligent Curiosity to ask further questions and seek out the truth of the matter.

Prove Yourself Wrong

Combat confirmation bias by setting a hypothesis then actively seeking out answers that prove it is wrong rather than seeking proof that it's right. This takes effort. Thomas Edison was once criticized for making ten thousand attempts to create a working light bulb. He told the critic, "I have not failed. I have simply discovered ten thousand ways that do not work." We're consciously going at the problem from the opposite perspective of the norm. Though challenging, the rewards are great. Develop a persistent desire to learn more about every problem you encounter and to weigh solutions from a 360-degree perspective.

A Motivational Speech

A prominent country club once called Jim Cathcart and asked if he would give a motivational speech to their staff of 25 managers. Since Jim belonged to that club he scheduled a more complete conversation about the goals of the meeting. The club manager said she wanted to motivate her staff to communicate better across departments. The tennis personnel weren't communicating with the golf personnel nor with the catering staff.

Jim's curiosity paid off. Once he examined the whole situation he realized that a single motivational speech would simply be like putting paint on rusted metal. It would still have the problem but temporarily it would look better. Instead of a speech Jim suggested that he should do a series of training programs for the entire employee organization of 225 people, including the landscaping department. The reason was so that everyone would feel more connected to each other and to the mission of the country club itself. Eight training programs were conducted over the course of the year and all employees were involved in some of the classes.

They worked together to create a custom training program for future employees. Various departments served on committees together and communication between departments improved dramatically! Club members frequently commented on the improvements. The general manager asked Jim to become a mentor to her and her two direct reports. What started as a one hour speech assignment became a year-long transformation for the club. Performance improved in every department and between departments.

An "edge" payoff for Jim was that he became friends with all of the 25 managers and many of the 200 employees. His member experiences at the club were upgraded in quality and enjoyment.

Intelligent Curiosity is at the Core of Success

For many, Intelligent Curiosity goes against the grain of their natural tendencies but that's what's required of success, isn't it? The application of Intelligent Curiosity requires extra effort, additional mindfulness and intentional interruption of the usual patterns of behavior.

Success is abnormal. Those who achieve the highest levels of success aren't taking the same actions as average people. They don't think the same way average people do. They don't associate exclusively with average people, either.

Achieving great success requires a certain abnormality of thought and action. Being successful is a mutant behavior. "Normal" processes don't create success. Intelligent Curiosity drives people to think and act creatively, to innovate. Ultimately, Intelligent Curiosity is at the core of success.

Intelligent Curiosity Causes Us to Look Beyond

When we are directed, focused, strategic and intentional we look beyond what is right in front of us. We don't just look at one thing. We look at everything that might affect that one thing. When we need answers to questions, rather than directly asking questions, we might reverse engineer how we go about getting answers. Start with the present and think backwards to the causes.

Let's take a simple scenario of a dog running down the street. We can ask why the dog is loose. We can ask where the dog is going. We can ask what the dog is running from or toward. We can ask whose dog it is. Or, we can consider a myriad of ways to catch the dog to prevent it from getting into traffic while remaining safe ourselves. If you like dogs you'll notice benign answers, if you don't like them then dogs will be seen as a threat or a problem. Each approach requires a different perspective, different questions and solutions. Situations like that often cause us to consider all of those approaches to a solution within seconds. We are being intelligently curious about the situation.

Beyond our curiosity is a level of situational awareness. We are taking in information from many different directions. Situational awareness is commonly taught in law enforcement and in self-defense classes. It's where all of your senses are switched on. It's a 360-degree awareness of both threats and opportunities. Officers are taught to always have a tactical response in mind--even when speaking with civilians. They're advised to keep a safe distance between them and others and be ready to make quick responses to any sort of physical threat. Civilians are taught to pay attention to their surroundings especially when walking to their cars in parking lots--not just for traffic safety but to be aware of potential threats. They're advised not to be talking on their phones while walking to their cars and to have their keys in hand among other things.

You may have noticed those who have been trained in situational awareness tend to sit with their backs to a wall or in a position where they can see everything and everyone around them. Their heads likely swivel upon entering a room, noting what's going on, who is there and even the location of exits.

Situational awareness can be applied to both personal and business situations--not just to personal safety. With a high level of awareness, you are more prepared to recognize opportunities others won't even notice. However, "seeing" opportunities is not enough. Being curious enough to investigate those opportunities is where success is often found.

Intelligent Curiosity Leads to Edge Learning

Intelligent Curiosity is not conventional curiosity where we find things to be "interesting." It's where we become deeply intrigued by not only what's directly in front of us but also to the periphery— the edges around the focus of our desire that very likely impact or influence it. We call this Edge Learning and Intelligent Curiosity is a key element of it. It's where you notice how things in the periphery impact the focus of your interest.

As an example, an entrepreneur's focus might be on the development of a single product or service. An Edge Learner widens their lens to see what other opportunities this product or service might create or what threats there may be against the development of the product or its need in the marketplace. This wide-angle lens creates situational awareness. Are there accessories that might make the product or service more useful such as protective cases and screen protectors for mobile phones? Are there other uses for the product that require a different type of marketing or to a different audience?

Google Glass was hailed as a societal breakthrough by making computer access and camera functions wearable in a pair of glasses. Jim Cathcart had the opportunity to test this technology in his role as Entrepreneur in Residence at the School of Management at California Lutheran University. Global news reports hailed Google Glass as a turning point product that would make personal computers obsolete. But at the edge of this wonderful new tool were some concerns that ultimately doomed it as a mainstream consumer product. People found the camera function creepy. They didn't want others walking around and recording them on camera without their permission or awareness. Google found strong acceptance of their product at the edges however. Industrial use of the product freed up workers' hands and allowed for more efficient recording, analysis and capture of data. Industrial operations could use the product among factory workers to increase productivity and nobody needed to be concerned about the camera.

Procter & Gamble launched their product *Febreze* as a cleansing spray that could remove bad smells such as cigarette smoke or pet odors from fabric. It bombed. People who live with bad smells every day often aren't even aware of them. Back to the drawing board! The developers decided instead to add a perfume to the product and market it as a spray to be used *after* cleaning. Instead of an "odor eliminator," it has sold very well as an "air freshener." It doesn't just cover up odors as other air fresheners do. It replaces them. If better questions hadn't been asked about the product, it may have ended up on the proverbial drawing room floor instead of generating millions in revenue for the company.

Similarly, Arm & Hammer Baking Soda has sold strongly as an odor removing product to be placed in refrigerators, though it was designed as a baking product. Who knew? Customers did and when the company observed what they were doing, they changed their marketing strategy.

Intelligently Curious People Become Thought Leaders

Those who develop and use Intelligent Curiosity in both their personal and business lives are more successful and they often become recognized as thought leaders. They're always asking questions and seeking knowledge from everyone they encounter. No matter their industry or level of financial success, they're always on the alert for new information and new ideas. They tune in to a frequency of greatness, their ability to dial in to problems and solutions and ask great questions is impressive. They think and notice at a higher level. They think like an owner or designer or creator, not just like a participant or observer.

Here are a few examples of questions we've heard from thought leaders when discussing situations we found ourselves in:

- What caused that to happen?
- Who or what was impacted by that situation and in what ways?
- What was the best solution and why?

- What advice do you have for others who encounter that situation?

Legendary thought leaders like master sales trainer Tom Hopkins and business expert Sharon Lechter dispense volumes of wisdom to entrepreneurs worldwide. However, when you meet with them one-on-one, they want to learn about you. They exercise Intelligent Curiosity in every encounter. Tom Hopkins is known to practice what he preaches. "When you're speaking, you can only deliver what you already know. When you ask questions of others, you are learning— gaining new knowledge that allows you to better understand them and their needs." Sharon Lechter says, "By asking questions of others, you demonstrate that you are truly "interested" in them which not only builds rapport, it also spurs learning and the exchange of ideas. It fuels creativity and innovation. This is the essence behind the phrase, be "interested" more than "interesting".

Intelligent Curiosity Drives Action

We also have a lot to learn about personal investigation from the innovators of our time. Take Buckminster Fuller, for example. Fuller is considered to be the Michelangelo of the 20th century. Amongst the many things he invented was the geodesic dome, which has revolutionized the world as both the strongest *and* lightest figure in all of architecture. How did he discover the structure of the geodesic dome? By studying the eye of a common housefly.

Fuller came by the studies of houseflies by first looking for what he called "the fingerprint of God." In other words, he was looking for patterns in nature. Essentially this kind of inquiry calls on us to discover more about how to do things *tomorrow* by learning and understanding more deeply about what already exists *today*. As Fuller studied the housefly, he noticed the shape of its eyes. He found that their eyes are a series of triangles. Triangles are the strongest geometric shape. How curious, that the eye of the housefly is made up of a series of tiny microscopic triangles!

Fuller took it a step further. He asked himself what would happen if he created a structure that mimicked the structure of the eye of a housefly using lightweight materials. What kind of pressure could such a structure withstand?

What he found was that it was miraculously workable. He built the geodesic dome and tested it a number of different ways, enabling structural and architectural feats that hadn't been previously realized.

Fuller described himself as **a comprehensive anticipatory design scientist**, and he meant it. Though he's most widely known for the geodesic dome, he also designed houses, cars, cities, maps, all with the purpose of doing more with less. He once spoke in an interview about his own brand of Intelligent Curiosity. Whenever Fuller frequented a newsstand, he would always purchase the magazine or newspaper in the upper right hand corner, no matter what it was. He said he did this because he wanted to know things he wouldn't learn otherwise. One day he might learn about cross country trekking. The next day he'd read about crochet methods. The day after that he learned about scientific breakthroughs of the 14th century. The day after that the subject was Scottish warfare. In doing this, he was able to see how different patterns emerged from seemingly unrelated fields, and the connections that might be drawn, from say, the eye of the common housefly.

It all comes back to this: Intelligent Curiosity drives action.

Intelligent Curiosity is a learnable skill. However, it requires commitment and ongoing practice. But do not mistake it for a trivial skill. It's a vital, complementary enhancement of other skills that are required to achieve success in all areas of life. It provides the insights necessary for envisioning innovation. It will help you recognize when to put ideas across, when to act and when not to act.

'Curiosity is the wick in the candle of learning.'
- William Arthur Ward

An idea is only ever just that, an idea, until someone takes consistent on-going action to move it from ideation to product or service. Lisa often hears people mention how they had thought of a successful product or service before someone else implemented it. They'd say, "but that was *my* idea." She then asks, "but did you take action on the idea, or did someone else take action on it before you?" Often the answer is someone else took action. It's the people that take consistent ongoing action that deserve the credit for taking an idea from ideation to implementation.

Down the Rabbit Hole

When you are practicing Intelligent Curiosity, information is a starting point, not an ending point. This most often looks like a critical engagement with the information you're provided; in other words, questions upon questions upon questions:

"What is the *source* of information?"

"What *premise* is this information based on?"

"How large is the *sample* size?"

"Do other primary sources *support* this claim?"

"Do I have *evidence* of my own to support or refute this claim?"

"Who does it *benefit* for this statement to be true?"

Source, Premise, Sample, Support, Evidence, Beneficiaries.

These questions have implications for your business pursuits, but they start with your day to day life. This line of inquiry boils down to, in essence, the scientific method:

1. Define the purpose. What am I trying to accomplish?
2. Construct the hypothesis. Here's the way to accomplish it.
3. Test the hypothesis and collect data. Is that reliable? Does it work? Is it the best choice?
4. Analyze the data. What can we learn from this?
5. Draw conclusions. What does this mean? And then what?
6. Communicate the results. Have I got news for you!

How often have you seen people jump from step 2 to step 5? We want our hypothesis to be right, because by extension that makes *us* right. Edge Learners trust that the process will lead you to the right outcome. And that sometimes, the right outcome is to be wrong, at least, every now and then.

When someone says "the science is settled", on any topic, you should realize that statement itself is wrong. Science is never settled! Scientific inquiry is perpetual.

Intelligent Curiosity is all about superimposing the scientific method on day to day living. What is driving your goals, whether they be business goals, or personal goals for your life? What do you think will help you achieve those goals? What questions will lead you to more questions and then lead you again to more questions? Don't panic if you find yourself farther out from your original question than you thought you'd be. Sometimes the rabbit holes we fall down are worth exploring for a little bit longer. Hey, for Alice the adventure only began *after* she stepped through the looking glass.

Implementing strategies of Intelligent Curiosity will help you more fully enjoy the roller coaster ride of business. It allows you to open your mind to new ideas, to pivot, transition and adapt as the marketplace requires. In fact, the Edge Learning skill of Intelligent Curiosity will lead you to celebrate the inevitable challenges or failures of life and capitalize on them.

Rather than walking away from stumbling blocks, you'll learn who put the blocks there and why. You'll make other people's stumbling blocks into your building blocks. The knowledge gained from Intelligent Curiosity will help you to move the blocks out of the way, climb over them, use them as building blocks, or on some occasions, choose an entirely different path.

.

TRY IT YOURSELF

Isolate a challenge or problem you are facing today. Write it on a separate piece of paper and then explore it by using the structure here:

"What is the *source* of information?"

"What *premise* is this information based on?"

"How large is the *sample* size?"

"Do other primary sources *support* this claim?"

"Do I have *evidence* of my own to support or refute this claim?"

"Who does it *benefit* for this statement to be true?"

Source, Premise, Sample, Support, Evidence, Beneficiaries.

CHAPTER 2

BECOMING AN ELIGIBLE RECEIVER

"Become the person who will attract what you want."
- Jim Cathcart

In the American game of football, there are 11 players on the offensive team. According to the rules, only six of those players can legally catch a forward pass. They're usually the ones who run the fastest and can get themselves out in the open on the field. They're known as eligible receivers. They have trained to both think and act fast. They are technically, physically and emotionally prepared to not just receive the ball, but to run with it. They are also operating within the rules of the game to assure that they are "eligible", meaning in the allowed position, at the time of opportunity.

Proper Planning Prevents Poor Performance.

The same strategy applies to business and to life in general. We need to intentionally open ourselves up to opportunities. We do this by preparing ourselves with technical skills in the fields that hold our interest. We open ourselves further by consistently working on the

Edge Learning mentioned in the previous chapter. This preparation allows us to recognize opportunities others might miss. It prepares us to create opportunities where none existed. And, it attracts new opportunities to us. Preparation, in essence, turns us into opportunity magnets!

Make Luck Seek You.

Have you ever noticed that certain people seem to get all the breaks? Some salespeople seem to generate leads for business effortlessly while others seem to spin their wheels. Some business professionals get promoted higher and higher while others get passed by. Some serial entrepreneurs create multiple successful businesses where others fail. The difference lies somewhat within their skillsets, but more often than not, they succeed because they have adopted the eligible receiver mindset. Start thinking of yourself as "lucky" and watch your luck improve.

The Mindset of an Eligible Receiver

One of the key elements of developing the mindset of an eligible receiver is expectation. Start your life, your career, relationships, your business with the expectation of good things to come from them, with them and because of them. Expect to meet the right people at the right time for the good of everyone involved. Expect great ideas to come to you. Expect resources to reveal themselves. This mindset will put you in a position to identify and actively pursue new opportunities. We will show you how.

Developing an attitude of service is another key element. Author, business man and motivational speaker T. Harv Eker suggests that to learn a new skill you should go to work for someone who is great at it already. Be an apprentice. Even do it for free! The lessons you'll learn from exposure to the skills of others will only enhance your own skills. This attitude of service will open your mind as well as opening doors to opportunities. As a young adult Jim Cathcart attended 400 volunteer service club meetings in a two year period working on community service projects in the Junior Chamber of Commerce, the Jaycees. All of these hours were unpaid but they were also the key to transforming him into an eligible receiver for the future he dreamed of-- learning and then teaching others how to achieve greater success in both business and personal relationships. He volunteered for leadership positions, served on committees led by others, worked on service projects, and attended every meeting he could in order to learn how to plan, lead, manage and achieve. People who aren't qualified or prepared usually don't get the opportunities offered to them. As a result of Jim's eagerness to do the work and to learn, he was rewarded with new opportunities.

Another aspect of an eligible receiver's mindset is ownership. They take ownership of every experience as to the creation of opportunities. In each experience they assume responsibility for the success of the event. They never think, "That's not my job." or "I don't get paid to do this." Instead they think, "How can I get this done? How can I help make this better?"

Be the First on the Scene

Lisa is notoriously early to events and meetings. She does this with the mindset of an eligible receiver. She introduces herself to and engages with everyone working at each event, expressing appreciation and enthusiasm for it. She wasn't always this way. In fact, the idea of walking into a room of strangers used to petrify her. Before understanding and developing her skills of Intelligent Curiosity she often left events she was supposed to attend without ever entering the room. Yet now, she watches for opportunities to be of assistance whether it's in organizing materials, arranging chairs, or inviting others who enter after her to grab a refreshment and find a seat. She is constantly looking for ways to take ownership in her experiences.

Think about it. When you arrive at a meeting, doesn't it seem natural to ask whoever was there ahead of you about what's already happened or what is going to happen? When you're the first to arrive, everyone who enters after you will think you know something they don't and they'll be attracted to you. They'll seek you out to gain their own footing within the scope of the meeting.

Lisa will often wear a unique hat when attending networking events because the hat is a great conversation starter. Demonstrating that she's open to such conversations positions her as being approachable, an eligible receiver. She will scan the room for signs of discomfort or isolation from individual participants and approach them, engaging them in conversation. She rarely approaches groups of people because they have already engaged and there will be less opportunity for a solo newcomer.

When Jim enters a room, he looks for opportunities to be of assistance, as well. He may offer to help the event organizers or to invite newcomers to find a seat with him, taking the lead in developing new relationships. He also makes a point of speaking to wallflowers, the shy people who would not initiate a conversation. And he always shows respect to the service staff.

Another aspect of an eligible receiver mindset is that they never turn it off. During her time as a private investigator, Lisa, expecting house guests, needed to pop by the grocery store for a few supplies. Always aware of her surroundings (through Intelligent Curiosity), she noticed a subject of an ongoing investigation in the next row of vehicles. This was not a typical location for this person to be, but receiving this opportunity to follow her was ideal. Had Lisa not been fully aware of her surroundings, only focusing on the task at hand, she would have missed that opportunity. During a grocery store run, she also completed an investigation assignment. Professional speaker Cavett Robert, founder of the National Speakers Association, often said, "School is never out for the pro." The same is true for Edge Learners, you're never completely off duty even though you might not be on the clock.

Eligible Receivers are Resourceful

Eligible receivers have the capacity and mindset to think outside the box and visualize the different possibilities and pathways for achieving their intended goal or outcome. When faced with a new challenge or problem, they actively seek out additional resources that will help them confront the challenge, and where they don't exist, create new resources.

When 'new,' or 'more' are not options, return to 'better.' Look at what's being made available to you and optimize it for your needs. Resourcefulness and innovation are not only about creating new things, but often start with making old things work better or more efficiently.

While working as Senior Program Manager at the United States Junior Chamber of Commerce National Headquarters, aka The Jaycees, early in his career, Jim recognized that though the staff officers, like himself, were constantly conducting training programs for others around the country, they weren't taking time to further train themselves. So, from a survey, Jim developed a list of topics that would benefit the staff and went to the Executive Director with his recommendations for additional training. These were courses specifically to fit the job duties expected from each staffer.

Though the Director agreed with the need and the topics he said there was no budget so the training couldn't be offered. So, Jim became more resourceful. He looked for new ways to get it for them. He surveyed the potential students and found that they were willing to show up early or stay late if the training was available.

Jim created a series of programs to be offered one hour before and after work over the ensuing months. He arranged for training materials using existing budgets and conducted the training himself for no pay. His colleagues loved it and eagerly participated. He also brought in guest speakers like a flight attendant from American Airlines who taught packing skills and travel tips. Even the Executive Director participated in some of the training! If the need is great enough, then be resourceful and find a solution. This dramatically advanced the way Jim was seen by his boss and his peers.

Rather than settling for the answer to "Can this be done?" Jim employed his resourcefulness to ask and answer, "How can this be done?"

Eligible Receivers are Adaptable

The entrepreneurial environment is unpredictable. Isn't that a great understatement? Most entrepreneurs compare their business lives to roller coasters--full of twists and turns and sometimes you just have to close your eyes and hang on. When you're working on the development of something new, it can be tricky to use standard practices, business plans, analytical tools and forecasting the way they were meant to be used. You have to learn how to adapt those tools to your specific situation. Or, in some cases, adapt your plans such that proven tools can be utilized to your advantage.

Learn How To Learn

Rather than being specialized and focused at a handful of things, business leaders are opting instead to become specialized at learning how to do new things. When Jim became partners for a few years with Tony Alessandra, PhD, he came to understand that getting one's doctoral degree was not about the acquisition of knowledge alone. It was more about learning how to learn and how to do research. Learners continue to advance "how" they learn in addition to what they learn. They become focused on what can be learned from everyone and every situation they encounter. Specialize in learning and adapting, then your world will open up with opportunities. The ball goes to the person who can best handle it or learn to handle it the most quickly.

Consider what experimentation looks like for you, not just in your product but in your process. Perhaps your services need to be modified or altered to suit a new clientele, or your business strategy needs a fresh set of eyes to revise how you approach the production and distribution of that service – what lies beyond the obvious? Look to the edges to learn more.

Get Outside of Your "Box"

Even look outside your industry for strategies that might apply to your business. Seeking answers only within your field is too limiting. A willingness to embrace and seek out new technologies, ideas or approaches will prepare you for the results of the opportunities that come your way.

Early in Jim's career he was hired by an insurance agency to become their in-house sales trainer and coach. The general agent who hired Jim said, "All of my colleagues in other agencies are looking only inside our industry for solutions. I want you to come here because you're not an insider. I want that greater perspective that comes from working with lots of different industries." For six years Jim worked with that agency bringing fresh ideas and strategies from his experiences in other industries. They went from last place in production to first among 125 agencies. They increased sales tenfold and won the President's Trophy twice!

Lisa was working on the development of software for those who attended conventions or training that applied to their fields to track and document their attendance and expenses. In Canada, business owners could attend and deduct expenses for two conventions a year related to their business as long as the convention was hosted by someone outside of the business. In the United States, a business owner could attend as many as they wanted. The criteria was that, if audited, you would prove that you actually attended and documented the meetings that took place. The software was used by business coaches and small business owners to record and provide the necessary documentation. As Lisa worked with business coaches and attendees alike, she realized that the content being offered at these meetings could be approved in a multitude of disciplines for continuing education credits. The content included both soft skills (Edge Learning) and technical skill training. The challenge within that industry was that the providers did not have a system or source for getting their courses accredited. By looking beyond the immediate need for tracking software to the accrediting sources that were in desperate need of content *to accredit*, the idea for Lisa's company, XTRAcredits, was born. This was an educational credits brokering service that connected subject matter experts to accrediting agencies, first by building a process to help identify and match their content to the competencies of the industry seeking the verification, then tracking attendance and providing verifiable proof of attendance for those needing professional development credits.

A secondary payoff was that Lisa was able to become friends and colleagues with many of the top names in the success achievement industry. New relationships led to new collaborations, and this book is one of them.

Assume that your existing practices are only second best and that you have yet to discover the best ways to do them. Ask, "Who is doing something like this better? How can I learn from them?" Be ready and willing to adapt to the ever-changing business environment. Lisa's experience as a private investigator absolutely required adaptation, often rapidly. She kept a trunk full of disguises to assist her with surveillance. She learned to quickly adapt her appearance, stride, body language and voice to suit each situation. In some cases, the disguises allowed her to forge relationships with her subjects, getting into character, to build trust in order to get to the truth.

Eligible Receivers are Relentless

It seems straightforward enough to say that if you're on a clear path to success, one roadblock or barrier would not be enough to stop you.

Well, what about two barriers? Three? A hundred?

When frustrations and fears build up in the face of constant roadblocks, how can you leverage your frustration to motivate you more deeply? What would it take to view setbacks not as failures, but as practice? John Ruskin said, "People have come to fear failure far too much these days. It is the practice necessary for success."

Coach Michael Burt, founder of Monster Producers, believes that we all have what he calls 'prey drive.' It's our internal instinctual ability to see something optically—either visually, or in our mind's eye—and have the activation and the intensity to flip the switch like an eagle after its prey. He has referred to Lisa as a pit bull for her tenacity to keep going after what she wants. Coach Burt recognizes that most people have a desire to achieve that level of intensity, but don't know how to consciously activate that drive.
The secret?

Allow the negative emotions that rise up in the face of constant setbacks to motivate you and drive you to persist further. Eagles are hunger-driven. Many successful people are driven by a hunger of their own. They decide what it will take to get there and intensely focus on achieving it. One more call. One more message. One more try. One more push. Whatever it takes to get you over the finish line.

"Whoever has the most conviction, gets the best outcomes."

- Lisa Patrick

What Ticks You Off?

More than one entrepreneurial venture was begun and driven by someone who was fed up with something. Their drive and motivation were to create the opposite of what they had previously experienced--something that frustrated them to no end. Many inventions have come about through a wish to avoid something or never to have to experience something again. Those inventors and entrepreneurs became relentless in their pursuit.

It is said that what makes a pit bull so menacing is not their size, strength or ferocity but their tenacity. When they bite onto an adversary they never let go. They just hang on until it surrenders or dies.

Figure out what you really want and then stay the course until you achieve it.

"Lisa is like a pit bull. When I say a pit bull, when she locks into something, she just keeps going and going."
– Coach Michael Burt

Eligible Receivers are Optimistic

When you are truly open to receiving, it is because you have confidence in your ability to take action upon what is received. You are optimistic about the outcome of the actions you'll take when opportunities present themselves (or are created).

Even when those actions do not produce the ideal results, eligible receivers accept the lessons that came with it. It's easy, when confronted with failure or rejection, to chalk it up to a personal failing. It's easy to beat ourselves up over missed opportunities. Such thinking does nothing more than put blinders on us against other opportunities that might present themselves. Eligible receivers know that. They acknowledge defeat, but only temporarily then give the world a 360-degree look through their new perspective of the lessons learned from the failure. And...they're back in position to receive the next opportunity.

Jim has been known to say, "There are Optimists and Pessimists, plus a third group who call themselves Realists. But, after much examination, I've found that the Realists are simply Pessimists who won't admit it! They always take a limited point of view."

Optimism is looking at reality and assuming that somewhere, somehow there is a way to the result you desire! It's not deluding yourself with unrealistic thinking. Instead, it is seeing your situation with all its limits and threats, and then seeking a different solution or opportunity to get there. There is truly always a way. It's not always wise to follow it based on cost vs outcome but there is always a way. Sometimes the "better way" might be too expensive or completely impractical, but if you aren't at least looking for solutions then you won't even see the ones that are easier, more realistic and practical.

On the other hand, pessimism is looking at reality and assuming that things won't change, and solutions won't be worth exploring. We suggest that optimism is the only healthy attitude.

Optimism is critical to being an eligible receiver—especially in the face of rejection or failure. Consciously practice positive thinking in the face of failure. Deploy Intelligent Curiosity by asking, "What opportunities are now available in light of this rejection or failure?" "What did I think or believe previously that is now proven otherwise?" "What else should I be considering?"

'Where opportunity is the goal, making yourself an eligible receiver is what will get you there.' - Lisa Patrick

TRY IT YOURSELF

What can you do differently to meet your next opportunity with more energy and enthusiasm? What have you discovered about your product, your business or yourself?

Ask yourself, what process or task can you revise to increase your impact in the short term? What structures are missing in your organization? What specific roles or responsibilities can be repurposed to achieve more? We tend to receive the opportunities that others perceive us to be qualified for. If they don't think we could handle it or understand it, then they look elsewhere. The more you prepare and grow, the more you are ready for.

"Optimism"

Think, Feel, Do
Think, Feel, Do
When you think you can, and when you think you can't
…you're right
It's a matter of mind not just a matter of might
To see it through your point of view is key
And you don't need to think the same as me
It seems completely plausible to say something's impossible
When you don't see how … you just assume - You Can't
But pessimism leads to less
The doubters don't clean up the mess
It takes no talent to tear others apart
The critic may be smart but has no heart.
Or you can choose to be among the Brave
The one who stands and faces every wave,
with certainty that peace and joy are near
if you only learn to look beyond your fear
Think, Feel, Do
If you think you could, you might
When you think you can, you're right
If you're pretty sure that somehow there's a way
Then you'll stay the course until you find
the success you hoped for in your mind
Hope sustains, Doubt refrains,
Dreams appear when we avoid the fear

What you think defines the way that you'll feel

If you doubt and criticize you'll make it real

But with Optimism you can make it so (Yes you can!)

You'll gain the strength to still get up and go

How you think is what you do

What you see can make things new

When you think you can or think you can't you're right

It's a matter of mind not just a matter of might

See what you want, feel the positive flow, think of the best

And Make It So!

Think, Feel, Do.

© Jim Cathcart 9-24-2014

CHAPTER 3

WHERE'S THE PROBLEM?

We lost a sale today and I'm not sure why. Our diagnosis was accurate, our price was fair, we have the ability to do the job and the customer needs it. But he didn't buy. Why not?

Sound familiar? OK, how about this one: *Jessie's attitude has been sour lately and I'm not sure why. She's usually cheerful and eager to help but lately she has been quiet or cynical. What do I do?*

How's this one: *Three times now the product has come back for corrections or additional repairs. We fixed it the first time so what's going wrong?*

The first part of solving any problem is defining the problem. What exactly is wrong and why is it that way? Our instinctive tendency is to start immediately solving problems without taking extra time to determine why they exist.

Be more curious! This can lead to even more problems and wasted time on the wrong solutions. Here is a way to look for the source of a problem so that you are more likely to resolve it for keeps.

What Is The Nature Of The Problem?

Is this a personal problem, a situational problem, an information problem or what? Until you determine the type of problem you are dealing with, you are not yet ready to properly resolve it.

Who "Owns" The Problem?

If Josh tells me, "We have a problem!" Do "We" really have one or is it mostly his issue?

Perhaps the problem doesn't directly affect you at all. In that case you are an advisor or assistant problem solver, but it's not "your" problem unless you assume ownership of it.

For example, if Hugo tells you about a problem with the landscaping project he's doing for you, it may be your problem at some point, but if it is not urgent to you yet, then it's still his problem. Solve it as an advisor, but don't take ownership of it unless you choose to.

Hugo: "Jim, we have a problem. The sod you wanted for the lawn is not going to be available for three more weeks."

Jim: "Will you still be able to install the sod then? Will it cost more?"

Hugo: "No, it will be the same cost and I'll be able to do the work then."

Jim: "I understand. Don't worry, just keep me posted if anything changes."

Problem resolved.

Suzy comes to you with a problem. "Boss, there is a guy on the phone insisting he speak with you, he won't tell me what this call is about, and I told him you weren't available until later today. He's being a real jerk about it. What do I do?"

Manager: (Take ownership of the problem to support your employee.) "Stay here and let me pick up the phone. Hello this is the manager; how can I help you?"

Caller: "Hey! I knew your subordinate was lying about you being available. Look, I want to tell you about an investment deal you're going to love."

Manager: "Excuse me. You were rude to my coworker and now you're being obnoxious to me. I respect my colleagues and resent your intrusion. Please never call here again!"

Suzy, who is now standing a bit taller and grinning from ear to ear: "Wow. Thanks Boss, that is a great solution."

Problem resolved.

To determine the nature of the problem, identify its origin.

Ask yourself, what is the source? Use the acronym "SPITS" as your formula for locating the cause of the problem.

S – Is this a **Situational** Problem? For example: if John was unable to process the paperwork at a government office today, is this a national holiday? Maybe all government offices are closed until tomorrow. If it's situational then don't worry about it, the situation will change.

P – Is it a **Personal** Problem? When Arturo isn't doing the work assigned to him, maybe he's feeling overwhelmed. Or maybe he is dealing with some personal issues that are daunting to him. It could also be an attitude problem if he needs another way of thinking about it. Address it at its source.

I – Is this an **Interpersonal** Problem? If the work performance is suffering, Jackie might have a conflict with you or someone else that is affecting the work. If so, the solution will involve two parties, not just Jackie.

T – This could be a **Technical** Problem. If someone gets wrong information or doesn't have the right tools or techniques to do the work, then problems will emerge. Don't blame or scold the person. Resolve this with tools, training or better information.

S – **Systems** sometimes cause problems. If you use the same system or process for multiple tasks, sometimes it might not work. Make sure that your methods are a good match to the outcomes you desire. Maybe doing things in a different sequence or at a different workstation or following a different protocol will get the desired results. Don't just follow the old ways because they're familiar.

So, you lost a sale and don't know why. Could it be that the customer didn't feel that you were interested in him or her? Just interested in the product or just following standard policies. If you are fixing the product and not fixing the customer's concerns, then you are overlooking a part of the problem. Too eager to get the payment, not eager enough to solve her problem?

Jennifer's recent bad attitude might be due to some problems at home (Personal) or from a financial crisis (Situational) or being overwhelmed by her workload (Technical or System). Don't assume it's any of these until you check further.

The boomerang product that keeps returning for another repair might be due to a faulty process of checking your finished work (System) or it could be something the customer is doing that is aggravating the repairs (Personal).

Once you become skilled at defining the source of your problems you will become much better at not only solving but also resolving them. SPITS is your guide to being more Intelligently Curious.

Yes or No?

Dr. Spencer Johnson, in his book Yes or No, The Guide to Better Decisions, separated choices into two categories: Personal decisions and Practical decisions. If something important had to be dealt with he'd assure that he used his head to ask practical questions and his heart to consider private or personal questions.

Practical questions included:

Am I meeting the Real Need? (Is it a want or a need?)

Am I informed of all my Options? (What information do I need?)

Have I thought it Through? (If I do this, then what?)

Personal questions included:

Am I being Honest with myself? (Am I telling myself the Truth?)

Do I trust my Intuition? (Does this feel right?)

Am I worthy of a Better solution? (Am I thinking big enough?)

Once he considered all of these, he'd revisit his decision and sometimes make a new decision.

Curiosity isn't just the emotion to want to know, Intelligent Curiosity is knowing how to learn what you need to know and to understand it well enough to use it wisely.

Are We Really Partners?

Jim was once a minority shareholder in a business partnership where he did all the revenue generation but only received a sales commission and none of the profits. He approached his partner and suggested that they restructure their deal so that Jim could earn equity. His partner would not consider changing their agreement. He said to Jim, "This agreement is working for me. The fact that it isn't meeting your needs is not my problem."

What is the nature of this problem? One part of it is Personal. Jim had no incentive to keep on growing the company because he was only compensated on sales, like an employee. Yet he had made a large financial investment as part owner of the business. Jim's problem? Not earning anything on his investment.

Implications? When someone has no incentive to go beyond, they tend to do only what is required. A lack of success motivation ensues.

Edge implications? This partnership was not a partnership. It was an employer-employee relationship and Jim was feeling exploited. If that continued, the partnership was doomed to fail.

The problem was not situational, technical nor systemic. It was personal for Jim and interpersonal due to the strained relationship between them. After much discussion, argument, tension, anxiety and frustration, Jim went to an attorney to seek a solution. The partner relationship was not repairable, so Jim wanted to recapture some of the money he had invested.

The attorney advised Jim that he was "in the right" and had a valid claim against his partner. He said, "We can go ahead with this, and you will probably win. But…it may not be worth it to you." Jim asked why. His answer was, "This will require a great deal of your time and attention. You will have to relive your frustrations many times before this is resolved. The time and energy you spend on this could be better spent on rebuilding your own business. This lawsuit will also cost a lot of money and any settlement you get will be slow in coming and smaller than you deserve. I suggest that you swallow this bitter pill of betrayal and just walk away. Sometimes retreat is smarter than revenge."

He was correct, it was a "bitter pill". When Jim realized the effect of this lawsuit on the rest of his business and life, he chose to just cut his losses and walk away. It took a few months to regain the excitement for growing his business, but once he allowed that emotional grieving process to naturally complete, he was back in the game and winning again.

Had Jim approached this as a technical problem and tried to resolve it in a courtroom, he would not have succeeded in doing what was best for himself. Who owned the problem? Jim did. His "partner" didn't care. At least, not until all sales stopped because Jim left the business.

Before that time and since, Jim has had many successful business partnerships and the scars from that one have now faded into obscurity.

Use your intelligent curiosity to determine whose problem this is and then solve the real problem, not the symptoms. Once the real problem is solved, all the symptoms go away.

Albert Einstein famously said "The important thing is not to stop questioning. Curiosity has its own reason for existing." For starters, you must be **curious** to even identify **problems** that are worth solving, as Jim has indicated.

SPITS places a focus on understanding the nature of the problem, putting edges around it, getting people thinking not in solutions but rather what is the actual problem that exists. Richard Branson, arguably one of the most successful entrepreneurs, has been noted for telling people, 'to launch a successful business means solving problems'. Richard asks intelligently curious questions long after other people have already stopped trying to discover the nature of the problem to find the solution.

It's been Lisa's younger-self's experience, have fallen prey to this at times, to identify the nature of the problem and then immediately want to solve it, by brute *pit-bull* force if need be. The challenge with this is that her innate sense of curiosity absolutely shuts down in favor of wanting to skip over the phase where a solution isn't immediately obvious.

Understanding the nature of the problem is **key to problem solving. When we activate our ability to be intelligently curious** – the process in which we are able to discover solutions (the result) once we have uncovered the true nature of the problem with SPITS - (the cause.)

When thinking about one of Lisa's new companies, Belongify – their mission is to help people "create connection" in their lives—Lisa realized very early that Belongify's path to success was more about the process, the intelligent curiosity about each other, than it is about what the process results in or the nature in which the problem exists.

It's More About The Journey Than The Destination.

Asking thoughtful questions that look beyond the obvious, seeing through things, opposed to JUST seeing things through, even challenging the status quo, or daring to wonder 'what could be different?' — this is what leads to creativity. The questions inspire creative answers. Without curiosity, there wouldn't be an opportunity for solutions, we'd just be accepting of 'it just is.'

'If you don't ask the questions, you'll never discover more."
- Lisa Patrick

Control is the variable in problem solving. **You can always choose to be curious.**

Solutions, on the other hand, aren't always necessarily within your control. You can try a solution even when you have discovered the nature of the problem, but if that solution doesn't work or that doesn't get the response or result you were looking for or intended - your "solutions" might cause other, unforeseen problems. The result of your effort isn't something you have unquestionable power over.

Curiosity absolutely leads to solutions. But when we focus on the nature of the problem and the journey; the intelligent curiosity advances us closer to what we want in ways that we'd never imagined.

TRY IT YOURSELF

Choose a challenge or problem you are facing or recently faced. Write it down.

Ask yourself, what kind of problem is this?

Who owns this problem? In other words, who is the most concerned about it and affected by it? Who else is directly impacted by it?

Should I advise or take ownership in this?

Is it **Situational, Personal, Interpersonal, Technical or Systemic?** Choose one.

Now design your solution or approach to resolving it.

CHAPTER 4

DIFFERENT TYPES OF PEOPLE
ARE CURIOUS DIFFERENTLY

'What we see, depends on what we look for.' - Lisa Patrick

People have always loved mysteries and admired those who solved them. Just as a kitten finds moving items and dark places irresistible, so are we with a "Whodunit?"

Our society is filled with both fictional and real heroes who solved the most puzzling problems and discovered things nobody else would have suspected. Sherlock Holmes, Charlie Chan, Mr. Wizard, Sergeant Friday, Nancy Drew, Mannix, Sergeant Preston, Rockford, Colombo, Perry Mason, Quincy MD, and many more were the dominant movie, TV, book and radio investigators of the Baby Boom generation. Then Scooby Doo, Magnum PI, MacGyver, NCIS, CSI, Bosch, Longmire, Blue Bloods, True Crime and Dateline came in for later generations. We love our crime solvers and inventors. Henry Ford, Thomas Edison, Jonas Salk, Richard Branson, Elon Musk... these folks don't think the same as most others.

The primary trait of all these diverse personalities, real and fictional, is that they have Intelligent Curiosity.

Though they were as different personally as anyone could be, they shared that wonderful attribute.

You can too. The goal of this chapter is to help you to recognize your own style, as well as to understand the styles of others, so you can apply Intelligent Curiosity most effectively to building relationships.

Which of these statements is most like you?

1. "If you don't ask, you don't get. Nothing happens until you take action and start probing."

2. "I can pretty much read people. Just engage them in conversation and keep it interesting. You'll find what you need to know if you keep them engaged."

3. "People will tell you what you need to know if you'll just give them space and be polite and patient."

4. "With a good questioning process all will be revealed. Start with broad questions and then be more specific. The system is the key."

Every person has a preferred style for applying their curiosity. We ask questions and explore information in the ways that are most naturally compatible with our own personality type.

- Some are bold and direct; some are polite and observant.
- Some are structured and precise, while others are dramatic and engaging. Which is you?
- Most say, "Well, it depends."

Yes, of course, circumstances and priorities affect what we do, but still, we all have a natural pattern to our behavior. That's how others "know" us. They observe our habits, our speech patterns, our reactions and our ways of doing things. Then they learn to predict how we would act.

Even our physical movements are identifiable. Jim recalls once seeing a former classmate at a school reunion from a block away. In an instant he knew who it was just by observing the way she walked and carried herself. Decades had passed since he'd last seen her, and he didn't know her all that well, but in a heartbeat, he recognized her! So, again, consider which of the four statements above is most like you, most of the time? Pick one.

Once you become aware of your own natural tendencies then you can learn to supplement or adapt your approach in order to be more effective. It's like our colleague, Lisa's current business partner and Jim's previous partner and friend Dr. Tony Alessandra says, "Don't just practice the Golden Rule (do unto others as you would have them do unto you). Also practice the Platinum Rule®, "Do unto others in the way that they want to be done unto." In other words, treat other people the way they want to be treated, not just the way you would want to be treated. To do that, you need to learn to quickly recognize their behavior type and understand how to relate to them. Some people are like you and you'll succeed in building relationships with little effort. Others are not like you at all and you'll need to adapt to their style if you want to gain their full cooperation. This doesn't mean that you fake your own personality to match theirs. Rather, it is to understand their styles and communicate the way they need to be communicated with.

Tension and Trust

The same is true when it comes to how you ask questions and how you explore your subject. The more suited your style is to your subject's style, the more readily they will open up and disclose what you need to know. Additionally, if your style is incompatible with another person's, then they might resist sharing information with you. **Your own natural approach to inquiry can limit what you find. If you always use the same approach, then much may escape your view.**

Two elements exist in every relationship, even the most limited ones. Tension and Trust. When you walk by someone on the street, if you don't know them, tension tends to be high and trust is low, unless something about them tells you that they are not a threat to you. When you meet in a boardroom, the behavioral differences in people tend to determine the degree of trust and cooperation that ensues. Even in existing relationships, when we don't understand how to adapt to the needs of the other person, tension increases and cooperation decreases.

What Causes Tension Between People?

We call this "Relationship Tension." Another form of tension is Task Tension. For example, if a fallen tree blocks your way, then the tension you experience will be task tension. The task of removing the tree and clearing your path is what threatens you. Once the task is completed, e.g., the tree is removed, then the tension about that goes away.

On the other hand, Relationship Tension is between people. If you don't like someone, judge them harshly, or they are being aggressive toward you, you will have anxiety about them or what they may do. Causes of Relationship Tension include bias, communication styles , language interpretation, assumptions about intent, arguing different premises, implied meanings, and basic assumptions.

For example, if you assume someone is your adversary then you'll approach them differently than if you assume they are your friend.

The key to winning with people is to recognize their style, be aware of your own style and learn to adapt to them as needed. Most people don't adapt, instead they try to get the other person to do so. Their (faulty) assumption is: "My style is the correct or best one and so they need to do things my way." Not a good formula for successful interaction.

Your Behavioral Style

Which of the four statements above did you choose to describe you? Which one is like you most of the time?

Statement 1 is the Dominant Director Pattern: "If you don't ask, you don't get. Nothing happens until you take action and start probing."

Statement 2 is the Influencer Socializer Pattern. "I can pretty much read people. Just engage them in conversation and keep it interesting. You'll find what you need to know if you keep them engaged."

Statement 3 is the Steady Relater Pattern. "People will tell you what you need to know if you'll just give them space and be polite and patient."

Statement 4 is the Conscientious Thinker Pattern. "With a good questioning process all will be revealed. Start with broad questions and then be more specific. The system is the key."

The way each pattern is revealed is through two separate dimensions of their behavior. You can actually observe the pattern in almost anyone.

Dimension 1: Directness.

Everyone has a place, a comfort zone, on the directness scale from Indirect to Direct. One who is direct will move rapidly toward their goal or task. They come across sometimes as blunt or bold. Their intent is to get the job done. They want closure or completion as soon as possible. When asking questions, they tend to get right to the point. Their pace is fast.

One who is more Indirect will be slower and more careful. Instead of "get the job *done*," their behavioral pattern will be one of wanting to get it done *right*. They are tentative and when unsure, they tend not to take action. Their pace is slower and more methodical or hesitant.

Here's the scale:

Indirect__A____B____C____D__Direct

Which position on this scale feels best in describing you? Choose a letter: A, B, C or D. Recognizing where you usually are on the scale is important to your ability to develop relationships that will lead to greater opportunities.

Dimension 2: Openness.

Ranging from Guarded to Open, this scale identifies one's priority: whether the Task comes first, or the Relationship comes first. Though both are important, one always is stronger than the other in the mind of the person. When the Task is stronger, the person tends to behave in a more guarded manner. They "play their cards close to the vest" and don't reveal much about their thoughts or feelings. When the Relationship is stronger, they tend to talk more, reveal more of their feelings, tell stories, give examples, reveal more. They put the focus on the connection between themselves and others before focusing on the task that brings you together.

Here's the scale:

Guarded__1_____2_____3_____4__Open

Which position on this scale usually feels best in describing you? Choose a number: 1, 2, 3 or 4.

You now have a letter and a number that reveals your natural behavioral style. Write it down. *Seriously, take a moment to write it down.* It will take on more meaning to you as we proceed.

The Direct styles are those who selected C or D.

The Indirect styles choose A or B.

The Open styles are those who selected 3 or 4.

The Guarded styles choose 1 or 2.

We display the scales in a grid like this

When displayed in this way, each quadrant describes one of the primary behavioral styles. Each behavioral style has a different way of engaging their curiosity. By their patterns you will know them.

The Indirect and Open style is **Steady** and called **The Relater**.

The Direct and Open style is **Influencer** and called **The Socializer**.

	VERY INDIRECT	SOMEWHAT INDIRECT		
INDIRECT	**A**	**B**	**C**	**D**	**DIRECT**
			SOMEWHAT DIRECT	VERY DIRECT

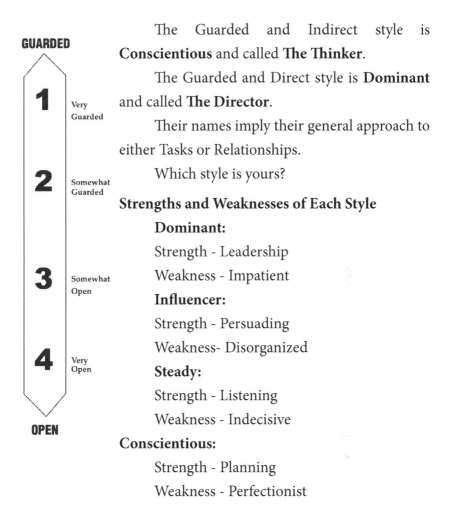

GUARDED

1 Very Guarded

2 Somewhat Guarded

3 Somewhat Open

4 Very Open

OPEN

The Guarded and Indirect style is **Conscientious** and called **The Thinker**.

The Guarded and Direct style is **Dominant** and called **The Director**.

Their names imply their general approach to either Tasks or Relationships.

Which style is yours?

Strengths and Weaknesses of Each Style

Dominant:

Strength - Leadership

Weakness - Impatient

Influencer:

Strength - Persuading

Weakness- Disorganized

Steady:

Strength - Listening

Weakness - Indecisive

Conscientious:

Strength - Planning

Weakness - Perfectionist

When people are like you, trust is easy to build. When they are not like you, tension tends to result. That's why it's not your style that matters most, instead it is your ability to adapt your style temporarily to become more compatible with the other person.

The more adaptable you are, the more they tend to trust you. The more they trust you, the more they will disclose the whole truth to you. If you want people to truthfully answer your queries, then learn to adapt your style as needed.

Happily, adapting is not all that hard. It's just a matter of adjusting either your pace (Directness) or your priority (Openness) for the moment.

- Put the Task first with Directors and Thinkers.
- Put the interaction (the Relationship) first with the Socializers and Relaters.
- Go slower and easier with Thinkers and Relaters.
- Go faster and more directly with Directors and Socializers.
- Make time for both parties to talk when with Socializers and Relaters.
- Make haste to get to the point, when with Directors and Thinkers.
- Directors just want to get things done and get on with it. Keep it focused.
- Socializers want to tell you what they think or feel. Keep it lively.
- Relaters want to be polite and considerate. Be a good listener.
- Thinkers want to be accurate and correct. Be rational and thorough.

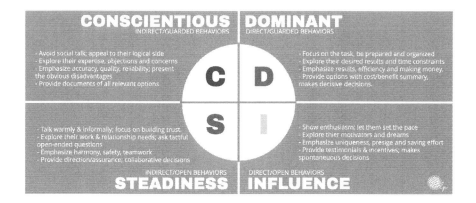

You may be thinking that this isn't always true. Situations change and people behave differently. That's correct, but *people* don't change. Behaviors temporarily shift, but the underlying behavioral style remains. Their emotional and logical needs are rooted in their main behavioral style. Learn to read people, observe their styles. Notice more of their directness and openness.

Lisa: For years I was adapting the style and patterns of my communication behavior to accommodate others without ever understanding what I was doing or why I was doing it, I just knew whatever it was that I was doing was working.

Until I met Dr. Tony Alessandra. I had never taken a personality style test, and for the most part didn't believe in them because I felt in my limited understanding of their purpose that they 'boxed' people into a set persona. I thought their determinations didn't account for how people's behaviors adapt and change over time or due to certain dynamic conditions.

One of the defining factors of my personal success is my network. By the way I think success is not defined by the dollar value of your bank account. That matters of course, but it's your responsibility to have more than one personal KPI (key performance indicator) of how YOU define success). The key to my success is my ability not only to quickly create connections with others, but to build equity with them over time.

People would make statements like, "Lisa you know everyone." Well, of course, that's just not true. The planet has over seven billion people and I most certainly don't know all of them. (But I know many more than most people do.) What's important to me is to invest in the people I do know without an expectation in return. My investment in them involves asking intelligent questions to determine what personality style they have so I can tailor my behavior, conversation and value to meet their needs and solve their problems. Doing so ultimately fosters connection and builds trust. I had been practicing the Platinum Rule® long before I ever even knew it existed. Now I'm even better at it.

Lisa is a Dominant Director. She loves the fast-paced world. She is task-oriented to get results. She is highly competitive and most often gets straight to the point, with very little filtering. She welcomes extreme criticism because she believes that is where she will discover more. She does not take offense to it. She *is* offended when someone holds back, but hates heated conversations. When they occur, she will retreat to handle those situations later with integrity and strategy.

Jim is a Dominant Director too but his secondary style is Interactive Socializer. In Jim's speaker role he is outgoing, interactive and entertaining. When focused on other tasks he is bottom line oriented and straight to the point. What he loves most is getting things done and doing them well. What irritates Jim the most is veiled truths, or white lies. He wants to know the truth now whether it is good or bad. That way he can do what is needed, even if that is for him to apologize.

In both cases, Jim and Lisa have developed their ability to adapt to others. They don't *change* their own style, they simply *modify* it situationally to reduce the gap with others. If someone is less assertive, they listen to them more and slow the pace. If someone is more open, they allow a bit more time for socializing or sharing feelings or thoughts before taking action. It's courtesy in action. As Tony Alessandra says, "Do unto others as they would like to be done unto."

Recognizing Behavioral Styles of Others

The problem most of us face is the lack of knowledge about the other person's style. How do we immediately get the insights necessary to know if the other person is one of the following personality styles?

- Director (Dominant)
- Socializer (Influencer)
- Thinker (Conscientious)
- Relater (Steadiness)

When we are intelligently curious and recognize these behavioral styles, we gain valuable insights into others including who they are and why they do what they do. These insights help us become more intentional and strategic about the way we ask our questions to discover more about them and potential opportunities.

Jim has been a professional speaker for over 40 years. In this capacity he has had to adapt to and understand 3,300 different audiences worldwide across virtually every industry and profession.

His ability to know what to wonder about and how to quickly gain an understanding of others in a different field from his own has been his most vital skill. It's not just his speaking skill that made him successful but rather it is his ability to understand and gain acceptance among complete strangers, day after day.

Lisa's ability to create connections with others is what made her a good private investigator. However, it was her ability to adapt, to be vulnerable in the moment to accommodate the other person's receiving style quickly that made her an exceptional one. She had to find ways to 'hack' the relationship because she was always limited in the time she had to spend with each subject to get the results that her clients were paying her for.

If you are looking to learn more about your personality style, you can find the DISC Profiler Deck, a new product that Lisa and Dr. Tony Alessandra created at www.DISCprofilerdeck.com or learn more details about your personality style at www.Assessments24x7.ca If you are looking to learn more about your children, you can go to www.KidsDISC.ca

Lisa's dad is a master at creating connections and being distinctively unforgettable. "My family lived 1,509 kilometers from my dad's family. For many years, we would pack up the car and make the road trip across Canada to visit my dad's family in Ontario. On every trip, without fail, when we would stop in some local diner or at a gas station to fill up, my dad would run into someone he knew. This became a running joke with us. "Who (and how many people) will Dad run into along the way?"

"I realized as an adult how valuable it was to have watched someone who was an expert at adapting his behaviors to others--utilizing Intelligent Curiosity--to create connections. There was never a moment, or at least that I can recall, that the other person would not know who he was. And my Mom and I used to get mad because Dad would stand there for 20 minutes talking and all Mom and I wanted to do was keep going. What I didn't know then, that I now know, Dad was asking intelligently curious questions and he wasn't doing all the talking but rather listening intently and gaining more reputation capital along the way."

Adapting your personality behaviors are the keys to the level of success you achieve in every relationship. Understanding your style while learning to quickly discover the styles of others and then applying Intelligent Curiosity to every communication is what will create new and greater opportunities for you all your life.

Be curious in the ways that are most needed by the situation and the people involved. Adapt when needed and refine your unique strength as well.

TRY IT YOURSELF

List four people you know.
Place each person on the Directness Scale with an ABC or D.

	VERY INDIRECT	SOMEWHAT INDIRECT		
INDIRECT	A	B	C	D	DIRECT
		SOMEWHAT DIRECT	VERY DIRECT	

GUARDED Then place them on the Openness Scale with a 123 or 4.

1 Very Guarded

2 Somewhat Guarded

NOTE WHICH STYLE THEY HAVE:
Director, Relater, Thinker or Socializer

3 Somewhat Open

Now write your primary style on the page and think about how the differences or similarities show in your dealings with them.

4 Very Open

OPEN

Please scan the code and discover your personality style. Get an entire report all about you.

CHAPTER 5

EDGE LEARNING

"The lake without the shoreline, the beaches
and coves is just a lot of water."
- Jim Cathcart

In Jim's 2020 book The Power Minute he describes the moment of opportunity between thinking about and acting on an idea. Edge Learning takes place in this opportunity gap.

No two people are alike. We all have different aptitudes and attitudes. We come from different backgrounds and experiences. Siblings raised in the same environment don't turn out exactly the same. We all respond differently to our environments. Some raised in loud and boisterous homes become shy while others wear the mantle of the outgoing with pride. Even when we share experiences and respond similarly, we often tell the tales of those experiences differently.

In Lisa's experience in police work and private investigation, it was interesting to hear the different perspectives of those involved in a common incident or how they would answer the same questions. Some would remember the make and models of cars. Others wouldn't have more than a vague idea of the color of a vehicle but would remember details of clothing including shoe styles. Yet others would describe body language or moods of those involved. We are all unique. That's what makes life fun and interesting. And it's the "how we are different" that matters most when working toward the fulfillment of our dreams and aspirations.

In this chapter, we're taking a deeper dive into what makes us stand out from the crowd; what makes us different; what gets us noticed and brings us opportunities others miss out on. The difference is in what we learn at the edges of our lives.

Edge Learning

Edge Learning is about how to be more intelligent and perceptive in every role you play in business and in life. Let's meet two young professionals: Zach and Wyatt. Both come from similar backgrounds. Let's say they both have middle class upbringings, parents who did not divorce, had the same number of siblings, and went to public schools. They both played sports fairly well and learned about being part of a team. Both went to the same college and earned the same degree. They even had similar grades. Both entered the workforce at the same time.

Now, let's move on down the road a few years. Zach sought out the companies with the greatest potential before applying for a position. His degree was in accounting but then he noticed that almost every major firm needs an accountant. So instead of seeking a position with only accounting firms, he also explored opportunities with other industries where he could add value as an accountant. He now has a great job with a thriving corporation in a field he had often dreamed of working in. He's so well-liked by his clients that he regularly receives offers to steal him away from that firm. He's on track to become the CFO in a few years. He enjoys his work, gets along with his co-workers and is often recognized by the leadership of the firm. Zach is always seeking new insights and curious about things. He always asks interesting questions that others hadn't thought to ask. He's a guy on the path to a great future.

Now, let's pop in on Wyatt's life. After graduation, he breathed a sigh of relief and took the first job he found in a recognized accounting firm. He didn't particularly want a career in such a firm but that's what his degree was in. While the company is growing, he is not. He doesn't challenge the status quo, he accepts it as is. He puts his head down and gets the job done well but doesn't seem to hear about other opportunities until someone else has been given them. Wyatt seems content to complete each day and go home to a comfortable routine. It hadn't occurred to him not to work for an accounting firm. He put his other dreams on hold and chose to just work this job until he could retire and do what he most enjoys. He will likely have an unremarkable career and remain average for the rest of his life. If that's what he wants, we have no challenge with that. But, if he lives a life of dissatisfaction and disappointment, he's nothing more than a bee in the hive. He could have had a different life.

What's the difference? Where did these two guys' paths diverge? Both were intently focused on learning the skills required of their chosen profession. However, Zach also paid attention to what was happening around the edges of that focus. Wyatt did not. Wyatt simply stopped being curious. When someone told Wyatt that he wasn't contributing to the growth of the firm. He said, "I guess you should've hired a better man." They replied, "We thought we did."

Notice the frames, not only the pictures. Growth Happens at the Edges.

A man was once accused of stealing art pieces from a gallery where he worked. They were losing money and suspected that he was the thief but they couldn't tell what pieces he was stealing. The owner challenged him each day as he departed and inspected his belongings. The accused always carried only one thing, a framed painting of his own. It wasn't very valuable but it was so nicely framed that it was quite attractive nonetheless. He had no apparent reason to bring it to work each day but he never failed to bring it along. Daily they would take his painting out of the frame to see if he had hidden another behind it. They found nothing. After a month of challenging inspections the employer finally relented. He said, "I give up! I know you are stealing from me but I don't know how you are doing it. If you tell me what you are doing then I won't prosecute you. Just satisfy my curiosity." The worker told him, "I'm not stealing artwork. I'm stealing picture frames." (Look to the edges, not just in the center.)

Edge Learning is the practice of intentionally redirecting your attention to the periphery to finding more. It involves seeing beyond the obvious; recognizing and acting upon opportunities beyond the expected.

"The average, see things through. Edge Learners, those that
are Distinctively Unforgettable - see through things."
- Lisa Patrick

Edge Learning is what helps differentiate you from everyone else with the same or similar training. Zach isn't just another accountant. He's always asking, "How else could this be done?" He's developed ancillary skills that allow him to showcase his skills and talents in the practice of accountancy. Those skills are helping him to find or create opportunities, build relationships and earn respect. He may not be dramatically above average in skill, but he knows how to find and create opportunities for growth.

When you assume that each day can be filled with new discoveries then you keep your eyes and ears open, you look around. When you know how to make connections with others, you'll expand your potential for the creation or attraction of new opportunities. You'll notice more and be noticed more. Showing up is a big deal. If you're not expanding your focus, opportunities won't even become visible to you.

As the Entrepreneur in Residence for the School of Management at California Lutheran University, Jim has had long relationships with the leaders and supporters of this fine institution. He is also a professor in their Executive MBA program. Several years ago, the University built an upscale "University Village" next door to the campus and created a wonderful environment for retirees and other successful people who wanted a simple lifestyle that allowed for active involvement with fellow achievers, thinkers, problem solvers, industry pioneers, authors and inventors. The Village holds education programs and discussion groups often including visiting professors and special guests.

While Lisa was visiting Jim and his wife, Paula, they invited her to join them at an event in the Village. She happily went along meeting many of the leaders of the group as well as the Dean of the School of Management. As Lisa tells it, that day had a profound impact on her life and career. Even though she was deeply involved in working on another project, she cleared her mind, making a decision to be present in the moment, making her an eligible receiver.

Lisa remembers looking around the room and thinking, "Wow, look at all the years of experience and wonderful stories in this room." She marveled at the wealth of information that would one day be forgotten. She was inspired to work with those nearing the end of their careers who are seeking ways to remain relevant and contribute to future generations in addition to her existing work with speakers and authors, emerging leaders, C-suite executives and entrepreneurs who want to amplify their brands.

Edge Learning is the continuous process of developing your peripheral skills--most often soft skills that impact *how* you do things rather than *what* you do. These skills are most often developed through real-world experiences, not in a classroom. This is something titans of industry, thought leaders and serial entrepreneurs have tapped into for ages. It's what makes one person with a great idea successful leaving the other with no opportunities to let their ideas fly.

Internal and External Edge Skills

Edge Learning is about how to be more intelligent at every role you play in business and in life. You will focus on the center, the target, the goal, knowing that your technical skills play a key role, but that your Edge skills are what increases your momentum.

Edge Learners understand that there are basically two types of skills necessary beyond what's needed in a specific academic field:

Internal and External. These skills are developed through intentional thoughts and actions around how they want to live their lives and who they want to become.

Internal Edge skills include:

- **Purpose.** Having a sense of purpose, whether large or small, whether we reach the objective or continue to strive for it, informs our existence and opens up the possibility for new opportunities. Purpose helps us to bring personal meaning and reach beyond our own existence.
- **Intelligent Curiosity.** Curiosity is simply wondering about things. But Intelligent Curiosity is wondering about the right things in the most productive way. It all starts with learning what to wonder about. It's about where to look when you don't even know yet what you are looking for.
- **Eligible receiver.** In life, we often get stuck in the rut of always doing the same thing. We restrict ourselves from trying new and different things. When we open ourselves to change, we give ourselves permission to explore more, do more and be more. We become ready, qualified, able and willing to act.
- **Confidence.** Confidence is not something you have, it's something you create. It comes from taking on tasks that challenge you and learning to adapt. Being confident is nothing more than a belief in yourself. It's a feeling of certainty. It's what gives you the power to move forward and take action.
- **Motivation.** Acting on your motives. A motive without action is a wish. Action without a motive is random behavior.

Remind yourself constantly of what you want and care about. This will keep you focused and motivated. When you know your motives, action will follow.

- **Being goal-oriented.** Most people are process-oriented instead of focused on what they want or the reason for doing it. Therefore they lose enthusiasm and miss opportunities . When your "why," your goal, is before you all the time, it keeps you moving toward what you want.

- **Accountability.** Holding yourself accountable is a conscious, deliberate choice. When you take accountability for the good and especially when you take ownership of the bad, you become trustworthy and people want to work with you.

- **Self-Awareness.** If you don't know how you come across to others, or realize why you are doing something then you'll be guided only by outcomes instead of being self-directed. Learn to notice your feelings and actions in every situation. Reflect often on what you did and why. Ask others regularly to give you honest feedback.

- **Belonging.** We are hardwired to long for connection. We learn to feel secure when we know that we have others around us who share our goals and care about our progress. When we feel we truly belong, we can show up as our real selves and contribute more fully to the group. An increased sense of self-worth helps us cope better when faced with stress.

- **Courage.** This involves taking action despite your fears. It is doing the right thing, keeping your moral compass in check and taking a stand consistent with your values. It's not always easy or natural. Perhaps the best way to think of courage is to treat it as a muscle. The more you use it, the stronger it gets.

- **Persistence.** No matter what we do in life there will be times when things go wrong and everything seems to be working against you. When this happens there is a natural tendency to do what is easy rather than what's necessary. The problem is most people don't stick with things long enough to realize the benefits. If you keep going, keep persistently moving forward toward your goal, even during times of adversity and difficulty, you will have a much greater probability of success.

- **Velocity.** This is a measure of your intensity and drive. Intensity is how hard and persistently you go after what you want. Drive is your level of desire for it. If you work hard but don't really care much then you'll give up too soon. If you want something desperately but don't work hard to get it, then it won't happen. Learn what your natural velocity is, then structure your plans accordingly.

- **Attitude.** Weak people are guided by their "moods" not understanding that they have a choice of how to feel about every situation. Your attitude is within your control. It is developed through point of view, mindset and way of looking at things. Be guided by your desired outcomes, not by your moods.

External Edge skills are those that impact how you interact with others in your work or personal realm of influence.

The external Edge skills include:

- **Networking.** This involves your ability to engage others in new relationships--both professional and personal. It requires highly developed soft skills, or interpersonal skills, as well as a strategic perspective. Your network is your breeding ground for opportunity. Strong contact networks provide highly focused opportunities.

- **Teamwork.** This includes your ability to work well with others, but be able to work independently at the same time for the goal of the team regardless of the situation. You must rely on your intuition to know when to listen and then when to contribute. When to lead and when to follow.

- **Brand management.** The ability to positively influence others begins with really knowing who you are and what you stand for (your brand essence). Brand management is about what you can provide to others. Your brand isn't about using the right logo and color scheme, it's about consistently showing up and providing an experience of transformation from surviving to thriving because of your knowledge and experience.

- **Persuasion.** This involves your ability to communicate with others in such a way as to convince them to carry out an action or agree with an idea. No matter what situation we may find ourselves in, persuasion usually plays a role in the outcome. Asking your kids to pick up their clothes, convincing a co-worker to take on a task, your boss to give you a promotion, or talking with a police officer to get yourself out of a speeding ticket, we all practice the art of persuasion.

- **Cultural etiquette.** This refers to knowing the guidelines for what is appropriate or inappropriate in communicating with people of a different culture. For instance in Japan, go ahead and slurp your noodles. Bow as a sign of respect. In Western culture, it's appropriate to shake hands. In Canada people take their shoes off when they enter someone's home. Expanding your knowledge of what is appropriate with people of each culture you encounter is powerful.

- **Relationship building.** Your ability to connect with others has a direct impact on your success. Curiosity allows us to learn about people, giving us a better basis on which to build rapport. Rapport builds trust. As Jim says, "A relationship is a direct connection between people in which value is exchanged." If there's no value exchanged, it's not yet a relationship. In Jim's signature concept of Relationship Selling, you treat the relationship as an asset. Money follows value. Give more value, receive more money. People don't buy products and services, they buy the solutions that those products provide from people they trust.

- **Leadership.** This involves getting people to do what needs to be done when it needs to be done even when they don't feel like doing it. The most important person to lead is yourself. If you can't lead yourself, then you aren't ready to lead others. People do what they want to do. Look for ways to make them want to do it.

- **Adaptive communication.** This is the ability to treat others as they want to be treated. When we appreciate the different personality styles of others, and we adapt to meet their needs our messages are listened to rather than merely heard. We don't have to change who we are, we just have to change how we behave in the moment.

- **Presentation Skills.** This is where you combine your communication skills to create and deliver a clear and effective presentation. It includes what is being said, how it's being said and what the benefits are to the listener. Public speaking is one of the most financially valuable executive skills.

- **Time management.** Time creation is impossible. God already created time. We must learn to use it intelligently. Manage your use of time. That means that anywhere we can free up more time for the important aspects of our lives, we will advance toward our goals. Constantly ask yourself, "What is the best use of my time right now?"

- **Sales.**
Having to sell a product or a service, does not have to cause you fear and discomfort. Not only can selling be something that you enjoy, but it can also be a highly profitable activity. The purpose of selling is to build profitable relationships. Without relationships there are only transactions, and every day is just as hard as the one before it. With stronger sales relationships every day will be easier, more profitable, and more fun! Sales is about creating capital. Being Intelligently Curious about others is how you grow the capital in your wallet.

"How" and "Why" - Which is More Important?

Author and optimist, Simon Sinek is most famous for the concepts in his book, "Start with Why." It is meant to be a book on leadership--how to motivate people through helping them understand why they are asked or tasked to do what they do at work. Jim is often quoted as saying, "The person who knows 'how' may have a job, but the person who knows 'why' will be their boss."

We want you to start with your own "why." Why do you do what you do? What is driving you down the path you're currently on? Before you can excel as an Edge Learner--before you'll put forth the effort required to develop your Edge skills--you need to know what *your* "why" is. If your "why" is unclear, *how* you do what you do may not matter at all.

Let's consider how Edge Learning skills make a difference in a typical networking situation. When it comes to networking events, most people show up with a pocket full of business cards or pens with their logo and contact information. Their entire focus is on giving out as many as they possibly can in as short a time as possible, believing they'll get business from them. You know who we're talking about-- the most obnoxious people in the room. "Here's my card. Let me know if you need to buy ....", "If you talk with anyone who needs _____, call me." Most of those cards will go in the trash can. Most of the pens will stay in the car or possibly make it to the junk drawer for all eternity never to be looked at again.

On the opposite end of the spectrum are those who do little more than hang around the refreshment table or make "friends" with people who have little to no interest or ability to work with them or provide leads for business. The "event" for them is just another waste of time.

Now, let's talk about how an Edge Learner might handle the same networking event. First of all, they have a goal in mind before arriving at the event. They enter the room with Intelligent Curiosity about the hosts and the guests who have been invited. They are friendly toward everyone, asking questions of each person they encounter. They exude confidence which draws people to them. They are eligible receivers. They may only meet one or two people with whom there is a connection, but those connections are likely viable opportunities.

Think about it. How do you become the most valuable person in the room? (Hint: Dale Carnegie had it right in his book "How to Win Friends and Influence People.") Take an interest in others.

"Thinking without action leads to missed opportunities."
- Lisa Patrick

You stand out through Edge Learning skills. When you think like an owner of the event, you *can* own the event. You can create opportunities for yourself that no one else would have even considered.

Here are some great tips to activate your opportunities at the next event you attend by using Edge skills:

1. Is there a registration desk or table? If so, how can you make yourself helpful in that area? Could the people there tell you where the action is or who to be sure to meet before you leave?

2. Is there a clear route to what happens before registration? Can you stand away a bit and direct traffic to that area? Could you greet and welcome people?

3. What happens after registration? Can you assist registrants with finding their way once checked in?

4. What conversation starters will you use? How will you show an active interest in them? Have you applied the 'Platinum Rule®'? (see chapter 3) How will you engage people to where they assume you know something they don't thus drawing them to you?

As an example, Lisa was invited to speak at a particular event. She arrived 30 minutes early, fully prepared. She had asked detailed questions in advance to know what was and wasn't happening at the event. What wasn't happening was that there was no photographer or videographer hired for it. Lisa went ahead and arranged for a videographer at her own expense to capture her presentation. Good for Lisa!

Even better for Lisa was that she recognized an opportunity to endear herself to the event hosts. She had more video and images captured at the event outside OF her presentation, so she could share them. She offered to send images to the event promoters for their use and to connect them with her resources the next time they held one. Lisa acted like part of the event team demonstrating the Edge Learning skills of communication, brand management, teamwork and relationship building. This led to Lisa assisting the hosts with other events, connecting other experts in her sphere of influence with them and more speaking opportunities for herself including a joint venture partnership with the host of that event.

By looking at the "edge" of opportunity at the initial event, she was accepted as "family" and made a distinctively unforgettable lasting impression.

Now You Apply It

Being an Edge Learner means that you have the skills to look beyond the initial circumstances and create opportunities for yourself. In this chapter, we discussed both internal and external Edge Learning skills. Part of being successful in business, and in life, is being aware of your strengths and weaknesses.

At the inaugural event for the Santa Barbara Acoustic Guitar Festival Jim and his son attended for the full day. The organizer was an expert in guitars and all things acoustic, but had only limited experience in organizing events. The experience was good but several small things made it awkward. Jim wondered, "Would the organizer be open to some suggestions to improve it?"

Toward the end of the day, Jim went to the organizer and suggested some easy and inexpensive ways to make the next event more enjoyable for the attendees and exhibitors. The organizer was so grateful that he asked Jim to serve as his advisor for the next year's festival. Jim ended up being a seminar presenter there. He spoke on "The Marketing of Art" and "The Art of Marketing." He met and became friends with many of the guitar makers he admired.

At the end of one of Jim's seminars in San Diego long ago, a man named Dr. Blaine Lee came up to congratulate Jim for a good presentation. He said, "That was really good, and I know some ways that it could be even better. Would you be interested in learning more about them?" Of course Jim was interested. That simple conversation led to many years of working with Dr. Lee and Jim's business grew in profitability. Dr. Lee earned tens of thousands of dollars from Jim and Cathcart Institute became more substantial due to Blaine's suggestions.

He was intelligently curious about how Jim could achieve even more success. Jim was curious as to how he could be his best. A match that worked well for both.

In this exercise, you will use the pyramid to identify your personal Edge Learning skills and prioritize their importance.

Get Workbook

IDENTIFY YOUR EDGE
LEARNING SKILLS

First, concentrate on your success, or the "why", behind the improvement of your edge learning skills. Write down a current goal or objective that you would like to reach. This will be the foundation for the Edge Learning skills you choose for each of the zones displayed.

Next, choose 5-6 skills to improve from the internal and external Edge Learning lists provided earlier in this chapter. Make sure that each skill is relevant to the goal you identified in the previous step.

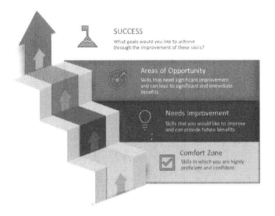

Use the pyramid to categorize your selected edge goals in terms of your comfort and proficiency. The skills you feel that you are proficient in will go in your Comfort Zone. These should be skills that you feel you are strong in and can use them easily when needed.

Edge Learning skills that are placed in the 'Needs Improvement' zone, are those that you may be functional in, however, you may not be fully proficient. It is important to recognize the opportunities presented with these skills.

The Edge Learning skills you place in the 'Areas of Opportunity' zone should be skills that will require you to push yourself and your abilities. These skills will ultimately put you closer to your goal but may make you very uncomfortable when focusing on them. It's important to be open and honest with yourself when choosing your edge learning skills.

After you've selected your Edge Learning skills for each zone, begin planning as to how you will work on these skills. To truly enhance your Edge Learning skills, it is best to practice them in real- world situations.

CHAPTER 6

SEEKING 360-DEGREE OPPORTUNITIES

What's in front of you? What is behind you? What is next to you? What is above you? What is under you? What is inside you or others? What came before you? What comes after you? What would happen if you did nothing?

It's our belief that the average person misses out on many opportunities nearly every day. They allow their current habits to control the flow of their days--even their conversations. Have you ever had an interesting conversation with someone and twenty minutes later exclaim, "Oh, shoot. I forgot to ask them about _____!" It's happened to all of us. The spark of a new idea was there but we didn't execute on it. Perhaps our conversation got sidetracked or we simply ran out of time. More likely, we were operating from habit rather than being truly present in the moment.

It happens.

But it happens less frequently to those who have developed skills related to Intelligent Curiosity. The intelligently curious are acutely more aware of their surroundings and of the directions of their conversations with others. They are more present. They listen more intently, and they are not afraid to ask questions. One of the secrets to success for the intelligently curious is to *keep* asking questions--even after getting initial answers.

A.T.W. - And Then What?

All changes have effects, some obvious, some not so obvious. All proposals and ideas have initial effects. The most successful ideas are weighed not only on their initial effects, but way beyond. In its simplest form the great value of curiosity is in continuing to ask questions about the impact of those effects.

Here's an example:

"Dad, I want my own money," said Jim's son, Jimmy, at age 13. "My friends get an allowance and I want one too." Jim wanted to grant his wish, but before arbitrarily giving his son a new income, Jim asked himself: "If I do this, then what?" The easy answer was that he would be providing his son, whom he loved dearly, with something that was important to him. It could have been a quick interaction and provided short term ease. When Jim asked himself "and then what," he started down a path of considering the long term value of the effects of providing an allowance.

An allowance would give Jimmy some discretionary money and a sense of freedom that was desirable for a young teen. It would be easy for Dad to provide, but it wouldn't necessarily teach Jimmy anything.

Jim decided to use this opportunity to teach his son how to think about and manage money. His financial education was a lot of work, but well worth it for the value it would have in his life overall. Jim agreed to the allowance but also to helping Jimmy develop good money habits.

At first, Jimmy was asked to keep a simple record of every financial gift, the allowance and every expenditure. That took awhile but the new habit slowly emerged. Once that was mastered, the next step was to learn goal setting, budgeting and saving. By the time Jimmy left for college, he had saved over $3,000 (on a monthly allowance of under $200) and his budget included him buying his own clothing, school supplies, dues and other things normally paid for by his parents. The long term answer to "and then what" was Jimmy developing wise money habits.

This strategy causes the person asking "and then what" to delve deeper into the possibilities for every potential venture whether personal or business. There's no negative aspect of delving deeper into what happens if we take the next step.

Another example from Jim's life was when his and Paula's first grandchild was born. They lived in the San Diego area at the time and the kids lived 220 miles away in Santa Barbara. The entire metroplex of Los Angeles lay between them--along with its infamous traffic challenges. Wanting to be involved in helping the kids and enjoying their grandchild, Jim and Paula endured the 440-mile round trip every week. It was miserable--hours spent in traffic jams. So, they considered moving. They weren't certain that moving all the way to Santa Barbara was the answer but possibly moving north of LA--the worst part of the drive.

The depth of consideration continued by repeatedly asking "and then what." With such a move then what happens to our business location? Our employees? Our suppliers? Our relationships with friends? Our involvement in our church? Our healthcare? One A.T.W.

wasn't enough to answer all the questions that needed to be addressed if we were to make such a move.

They thought it through, talked with the employees, helped them relocate, outsourced many services and saved over $200,000 a year in operating costs by moving to Thousand Oaks, north of L.A. They cut hours from their trips to visit with the kids and were able to establish all new connections. The "and then what" questions served them well again more recently (19 years later) as they moved from California to Texas. The big take away from those three simple words is how you can determine if the payoff is worth the pursuit of the proposal. Is the juice worth the squeeze?

What will that do to your day-to-day life?

When Jim was partnered with Dr. Tony Alessandra in Cathcart, Alessandra and Associates, Tony took a call from AT&T. They were seeking a training design company to do a custom project that involved topics outside of Jim and Tony's expertise, but it would generate a six figure fee. It was very tempting because they could have done it, but it would have taken them away from their main business and later on it would have cost them even more than it made due to missed opportunities. Reluctantly, they declined the opportunity. In reflection, they were glad they did.

At age 30 Jim had decided to become a full-time professional speaker. His role models were Earl Nightingale, Cavett Robert, Bill Gove and Dr. Kenneth McFarland, all speakers, authors and very busy travelers. In fact, Cavett Robert and Bill Gove, founders of the National Speakers Association, were traveling to more than 200 conventions and meetings every year! That is the career Jim wanted.

Around this time, a friend invited Jim to go golfing with him. He really enjoyed the game, so he bought a small set of golf clubs and a roller cart plus some balls, gloves, and tees. He was "getting into golfing." Then, in a valuable moment of reflection, he asked, "OK, if I become a golfer...and then what?" Golf is a game that requires equipment, locations and practice. You need a golf course, a set of clubs, maybe a cart, a golf teacher, and at least three or more hours of time just to play one game. Jim's new career path didn't afford him that kind of time-luxury, nor did he want to ship golf clubs wherever he went.

Instead of golf, Jim chose to take up jogging. He sold his golf ensemble to a friend and walked away. Yes, he could have found a way to incorporate golf into his life, but it was much easier to take up running instead. Jim has run all over the world since then and loved every mile of it.

Think about the most important parts of your life, isolate the major decisions you might be facing in each. Choose a path and then pose the question, "And Then What?" At least three times. If you choose to go ahead and then what? If that next step is taken, and then what? If *that* action is taken, and then what? If you don't like the answers you get, choose a different path.

Surviving vs. Thriving

One of the keys to survival as human beings is our dependence on each other. We *need* other people. We need them to create products and services that we depend on. We need them to build homes, lay roads, build and repair infrastructure, grow and transport food, provide electricity, water and, yes, internet services. To achieve beyond the average in life, we need to create the relationships that will help us to not only survive, but to thrive and prosper.

Those who are most successful in life have become experts at creating opportunities. They seek out and take advantage of educational opportunities. They become proficient in the skills required to build relationships with others. They are directed, focused, strategic and intentional. And, they are quick to determine which "others" are best to build those relationships with. They have developed a 360-degree awareness of thrival opportunities.

We can learn from anyone we encounter, on or off the job. Have you ever had a random conversation with a stranger who imparted a bit of advice that served you well?

Oops!

Once Jim and his wife took their very young son to a restaurant. The hostess asked, "How many are in your party?" Jim jokingly replied, "Two and a half." The hostess then knelt down to their son's eye level and said, "He looks like a whole person to me." Then she smiled and asked the server for a table for three.

Jim was a bit embarrassed by his off-handed remark of "two and a half" and never again referred to a child as anything other than a full person worthy of full recognition and attention.

Lisa's experience was quite different, but made a huge impact just the same. She was the youngest person on the Board of The Private Investigators of Alberta. She was also the only female and fully dedicated to her craft. She had honed her skills of blending in--creating personas to suit each case and being forgettable in public arenas which enhanced her ability to get the information she needed and move on.

Another board member, David Rodwell, retired investigator, major crimes division of the Royal Canadian Mounted Police, invited her to an event where professional presentation coach and Hall of Fame professional speaker, Patricia Fripp would be speaking. Lisa was baffled--wondering how she could benefit from learning about public speaking when her goals were most often not to be seen, heard or remembered.

However, her belief that a missed opportunity was "no opportunity" won out. When Patricia entered the room and began speaking, Lisa was overwhelmed by the impact of her presentation. It was as if this five-foot, two-inch dynamo was speaking directly to her. Lisa realized that day the power of public speaking and how to make others feel important through presentation skills. She also formed a professional friendship with Miss Fripp.

Now, you may want to attribute some of those situations to fate or circumstance, but we know they would not have occurred had we not developed our own 360-degree awareness for opportunities to help us thrive.

Most people put up protective barriers to creating new relationships with their prospective customers and others around them. They are apprehensive of having others get too close. That's a survival instinct. We learn it as children when we are told not to talk to strangers. To thrive in life, we need to be aware of that protective instinct, of course, but to open ourselves up to the three stages of building relationships. Those three stages are:

1. Curiosity
2. Information
3. Commitment

Developing your skills in each of those stages is a starting point of Intelligent Curiosity.

Take a Lesson from Law Enforcement

We referred earlier in the book to how those in law enforcement take training to increase their awareness of surroundings and situations. Jim has interviewed members of law enforcement, including state police officers, undercover officers and Texas Rangers. They talked about how they were intentional about how they observed and explored situations. They don't just focus on a scene. They are trained to take in everything surrounding the scenes, including what doesn't fit and what might be missing, or doesn't belong. This is the essence of Intelligent Curiosity.

As a private investigator, Lisa had to learn to ask questions differently or to ask the same question in different ways. After all, she was hired to gather information on people quite unlike herself. She had to learn to question every move they made, every interaction they had with others, their patterns of behaviour and routines to discover the facts necessary to get the job done. She was constantly switching from making broad scans of situations to picking up on smaller, specific details that pointed to the truth of the matter.

Both criminal and private investigators work diligently to explore multiple avenues to capture the answers they need and to work toward the results they hope to achieve.

Become a Personal Investigator

We are suggesting that you develop similar skills in order to become a *personal investigator.* Draw inspiration from the tactics used by intelligence agencies, criminal investigative work and investigative journalism to provide different lenses through which to view your 360-degree surroundings to seek out new opportunities.

- Uncover more of what your customers really think and feel
- Learn more about your business associates and employees, including insights they have about your business
- Engage in productive conversations with those outside of your industry, seeking new ideas or strategies
- Seek out new relationships for what you may become exposed to or new knowledge you'll gain
- Learn to switch seamlessly between being highly focused and then scanning, seeing what's happening at the edges of every situation

Lisa does a lot of brand work with her clients. It's the nature of her work to build trust in relationships and to come to understand their needs and expectations. Analyzing their expectations for their brands requires her to view the brands from two perspectives:

1. From her client's point of view and
2. From their client's point of view, the perspective of that brand's potential customers.

One of the biggest mistakes she sees both new and seasoned brands make is to be highly focused on *the person behind the product* rather than what the product will do for the clients. In some cases, there's no evidence of being aware of the needs of the buying audience.

"Hire me because I'm an amazing person!" That's what many websites seem to say.

Too many personal service websites are all about the person and their message instead of focusing on what the prospective client is seeking. The thought leaders who excel at client engagement consider the benefits of their product from all angles then focus their messages on what their intended audience is struggling with and the solutions they provide--how they help their clients from where they are today to where they want to go. From survival to thriving. THAT is how they create opportunities where there were none before!

For example, on a doctor's website Lisa was working with, the overall message was to "Find peace. Even in the barren places." The image on the page was of a desert with sand dunes. And the CTA (call to action) was to "Take the Journey." Before delving deeper, Lisa felt moved to ask jokingly how their ATV (all-terrain vehicle) sales were, as that's what came to mind from the message the site was presenting. After asking a series of intelligently curious questions, Lisa was able to uncover what the doctor really wanted her potential clients to see, think and feel about her services as well as the next action to take. When we speak too metaphorically in our marketing, often the intended client won't understand what we can do for them. She was able to create a valid opportunity to help her client improve the results she was getting online.

One of Jim's favorite colleagues, Lisa Marie David, had a training company called "Winning Waves." She loved the sea and the metaphor seemed perfect to her, as the waves of life can flow and change. Her graphics showed ocean scenes. Pretty, but it meant nothing to her intended clients. After speaking to several of her customers, she saw the solution was simple: change two letters in the second word. Make it "Winning Ways." It was perfect! That is what she teaches and now her clients can see what she is all about, in a catchy phrase.

When you become more aware, focused and intentional rather than going through life on auto-pilot, you'll be amazed at how many opportunities you have walked by in the past. You'll gain a new perspective on your own potential for success and gain greater satisfaction in all the relationships you develop. Remember, everyone you meet has their own sphere of influence and could potentially connect you with someone you've been waiting your whole life to engage with!

TRY IT YOURSELF

To enhance your 360-Degree Awareness

———————— Let's apply this to your situation right now.

Choose a situation you want to focus on, then:

- What is obvious? Notice everything that requires no extra effort nor interpretation. What do you see, hear and feel? Notice more, look again.
- What could this mean? (Not what 'does' it mean, but what 'could' it mean?)
- What caused this?
- Who is connected to this? Who benefits or loses from this?
- What is adjacent to this?
  What's on the Edges? Not necessarily related but still nearby.
- What else is like this?
- And finally, ask, what is missing from this?

CHAPTER 7

WHAT IS YOUR SUCCESS VELOCITY™?

*If you don't care where you are going
it won't matter how fast you travel.*

Do more, faster and better with less. That's the mantra: More productivity, more effort, more results — the list of requirements in business seems to never end. Whether you're a business owner sitting in the C-Suite, a small business owner, or a solopreneur; everyone is faced with an enormous amount of pressure every day just to keep up with the status quo.

This is where your curiosity may need to be redirected. Most people just focus on working harder, to put more effort or force into what they are doing. Some focus on working smarter, being more efficient in their efforts. But sometimes it makes sense to question whether what we are doing is truly contributing to our business and whether it might make sense to sometimes do even less.

Anything worth doing is worth doing poorly at first. Perfection is a great goal but learning and growth are also important. Some things must always be done exactly right, as when safety is a factor. But many things can be done awkwardly for a while and then improved as we grow. Also, giving your full effort isn't always your best practice. If you are more effective at a pace or effort that is lower than your maximum, then maybe "Optimum" is your better goal.

We are always striving to do better than we have previously done. We set goals that we believe will enable us to succeed.

We have found that when a goal is more personal — that is, it comes from our own motivations rather than being set for us by someone else — we're more likely to achieve that goal.

In essence, all that is required to create and achieve your goals is focus, hard-work, determination, persistence, knowledge, micro-milestones and velocity.

We are all hard-wired to want more, be more and achieve more. What defines 'more' looks different for everyone. It's easy to think that the more work, the more we take on and the faster we do it, the more successful we will become. Just because you are moving fast, does not mean you are moving forward.

Speed vs Velocity

Let's take NASCAR as an example. If a car is going 200 miles an hour, its speed is 200 miles an hour. If there is no race that day, its velocity is zero. **Velocity means the rate of advancement toward the target or goal.** In other words, it is how quickly you make progress toward a desired outcome or destination.

Personal **Velocity is your rate of advancement toward** *your* **desired outcome.** Regardless what your intended goal happens to be, every person has a natural velocity – an intensity and drive that is natural to you.

Trying to increase your velocity can be a slippery slope. We live in an age where burnout is so common that it is sometimes celebrated as a hallmark of success, and depression a sign of weakness.

Drive is the desire, the zeal, the commitment, the "all in" - that psychological factor. It is like torque, or the force. I may be physically able to do a mountain hike really intensely and sustain the exertion to go up the hill at a rapid speed, but if I don't have the drive to endure the pain, I'm going to back off. Likewise, in business. I might have the wherewithal to get it done, but if my drive isn't strong enough, then I am likely to give up early.

Things That Are Measured Tend To Improve.

To increase your Drive, clarify your "why." Spend time reviewing your goals and dreams. See the clear connection between what you will do and why it matters to you or your company. Become more self-aware. Keep numbers or stats on where you are in relation to your goals. Create a wall chart, get an app, find a way to know where you stand daily or even hourly. Visualize yourself achieving your goal. Carry a description of your goal in your wallet, purse or backpack and look at it often.

Intensity is activated by your Drive and it is about sustaining your energy, your strength, your endurance. **Drive is the want to, Intensity is the effort.** They are aspects of your life that can be improved, or that can deteriorate through neglect. You can improve intensity with training, good nutrition, adequate amount of rest and the right kind of nourishment and exercise. There are many things you can do to increase your ability to sustain intense effort.

Everybody has the ability to increase their intensity somewhat, but not everybody will know how to manage their intensity to stay in *the zone that is right for them.*

Finding Your Zone

Your zone of intensity ranges between: asleep on the low end or fully engaged on the high end, but there's a range within those limits that is natural for you.

Jim's example: I'm five feet nine inches tall, and I weigh 150 pounds. There's only so much my body's physically capable off. I'm over 70 years old now, so I'm physically limited because my body has changed over time, but other parts of me are still strong and vital. So if I decide to become an acrobat, I've got a dysfunctional goal and a darned hard road ahead of me. Maybe I could do it, but I'll die in the process. I will break bones. I will go through misery and grief. It is the wrong goal for me. I need to know what is the optimum, the natural zone of velocity for me - my ideal intensity.

Combine intensity and drive – and we've got what Jim calls the ingredients for making the perfect milkshake. When intensity and drive are mixed together, we're making the milkshake he calls personal velocity.

Lisa: Let's take a deeper look at intensity. My zone of intensity is naturally high even when I am going about life in my usual way. Even when I'm relaxed, I'm more intense than the people around me. When I'm going at a slow, easy pace, I'm still walking faster than the other people, not just because I'm physically stronger, but because that feels right to me. So I have to consciously slow down to stay with the other people if we're just walking through a mall.

That's how I adapt my personal natural velocity to fit those around me and the circumstances I'm in.

The same thing holds true on the job. Some people go immediately to work and they start juggling tasks, often multi-tasking – they may have up to 15 things going on. People that gravitate towards this tendency are happy to do it! Other people come in, grab their coffee, socialize with others and take their time before they ever sit down at their desk. In the South we call this "fixing to go to work."

People with low velocity tend to be very comfortable with a slow pace that doesn't require sustained effort. They seek energy from outside themselves, from other people. And the high end of their velocity zone isn't very high.

It's high enough to get through life successfully. They could occasionally compete in some kind of a challenge and do just fine, but they wouldn't be able to sustain high velocity over time without risking burnout.

Anybody can go at bursts of high intensity. But that doesn't mean their natural velocity is any different. I trained for a half marathon and was able to do it and succeed, but only specific to that goal. That was my personal best at the time and I probably won't do it again.

Someone with a higher natural velocity would be able to sustain it multiple times over extended time.

Dean Karnazes embarked on the well-publicized Endurance 50: 50 marathons in 50 states in 50 consecutive days. When I first heard about this journey, three things came to mind. First, I didn't even know that was humanly physically possible. Second, where does his drive come from? And third – Dean has epic velocity!

His velocity would have to be among the highest of all humans who've ever lived. And that's okay. Nobody that I could think of should want to be like him. But everyone should want to learn something from him. Because he has a lot to offer.

Imagine the people around you. Think of their levels of velocity like a metronome, the clicking device that keeps timing for music, the beat. Some are faster, some are not. But everyone has a natural velocity, a zone in which they are at their best for the circumstances. The right rhythm for one song might be the worst for another. Playing a song faster doesn't make it better, especially if it is a waltz. The same is true for people.

Velocity can be observed in anybody, all you need is more than a moment to observe it, because if all you observe is a moment, you don't have a clue what their velocity is.

In a singular moment, all you see is the adaptation happening in that moment. You don't know if it can be sustained or if it's natural. So snapshots aren't helpful. It's the difference between a photo and a video – in a video, you're getting the sense of a person's patterns of behaviour.

Take jogging for example. Let's say your normal heartbeat is 60. As you jog, it may go up to 140. That's great for a workout. But you can't do that all day. And if you do that all day, you will harm your body.

How Can You Discover Somebody's Personal Velocity?

Observe their patterns.

Exercise: Choose a person to focus on.

Notice how big their goals are, what size of challenges

they are energized by or overwhelmed by. Notice the pace they set for themselves. Notice what they do for leisure; more activity or more relaxation. How quickly do they begin a task? How long did they sustain their effort before feeling that they need a break? Or a distraction?

How many things are they juggling at one time happily?

The qualifier is whether or not they are managing happily. Because it could be harming them. A person with high velocity actively seeks out more - the minute they get control of a task or project (not the completion of that task, just the control of it), they'll immediately pick up something else to increase the difficulty or the resistance because they thrive on the resistance. It's the push back that they want.

"If I don't struggle, I won't improve."

When Jim was in China, he was sitting at the big dinner table with the food in the center and he reached with his chopsticks to serve himself. He was struggling because it was new to be using chopsticks. Two or three people immediately said, "Here, let me get that for you!" Their offer signaled that, because Jim was the teacher, he was to be served not just not to serve myself. And he said, "No, no. If I don't struggle, I don't improve." They stopped. And they thought about that, and then they saluted Jim. They acknowledged it. They told Jim, "I get it. What an admirable thing to say. Yes, teacher. Go ahead and struggle." So Jim struggled until he got to be pretty good with chopsticks.

Now when Jim goes into a new situation, in the first few moments, he's scoping it out to see what he can learn to do. For him, it's not enough to just do it. He's always looking to do it better.

An Edge Learner seeks to discover the limits of their own natural velocity. Because here's a thing about velocity: if there's not enough challenge, you'll inevitably go into a very predictable decline. First, you'll experience boredom. Second is apathy. That's where you stop caring. Finally, apathy leads to depression. People need a sense of purpose; they need to care.

If people don't care, that's a symptom of an underlying disorder. They need to care.

So if you are not challenged enough, then first comes boredom. Second comes apathy. You've been bored for too long, and now you no longer care. Third is depression. When you reach depression, that's clinical. We don't necessarily mean that you have to physically attend a clinic, but it could be the case depending on the circumstance. What we mean is that it's reached a clinical level as a problem, which means you have to go through a recovery cycle just to get back to normal.

Never Too Little, Never Too Much, Stay In Your Zone

Your natural velocity is not a setting, it is a zone with an upper and lower limit to your effectiveness. So it's never a good idea to under-challenge yourself, even if your velocity is low. Nor is it sensible to over challenge yourself.

Another example of low velocity: Jim was doing a seminar on this. He profiled all the people in the audience using a questionnaire, and this one man came out with very low natural velocity.

The audience member at Jim's seminar said, "I work on the trading floor of the New York Stock Exchange." Jim asked, "How do you feel about that?" He said, "I love it. It's thrilling. But when I go home, at the end of the day, I have to take a stiff drink and lie down and not talk to the family for a while."

This is a guy with low velocity who was able each day to put himself in a high velocity situation at work. At the end of the day, it wore him out. Now if he did that for multiple years, he would end up with physical ailments and psychological problems and would have to go through a recovery cycle just to have a normal life. He could do that for a short burst of time, yes, but he was in the wrong job.

He needed to have a job that would allow him to occasionally go down on the trading floor, be involved to his full desire and capacity, and then get the heck back to a quiet office routine.

The upper end of velocity is reached when you push yourself too much, when the challenge is too great and could cause psychological or physical harm. The first symptom you'll feel is nervousness or stress. It might be followed by anxiety. It will certainly ultimately lead to burnout.

Nervousness is just what happens when your nerves are on edge. It's a high level of physical agitation. Anxiety is based in fear, so anxiety is fear-based eagerness, which is the opposite of motivation. It might be experienced at the same level of intensity as eagerness sometimes, but eagerness is based in anticipation and desire, whereas anxiety is based in dread and fear.

Eagerness and anxiousness are similar, but eagerness is healthy, because it stimulates HDL cholesterol, or healthy cholesterol. Anxiety stimulates LDL, the lethal cholesterol which is based in fear.

So your nervousness turns into anxiety or starts eating away at your eagerness. If you continue for long, by pushing too much, taking on too much, having too many balls in the air at one time, too many people coming to you asking for upcoming deadlines - you achieve burnout.

And burnout is like depression on the other end. It's the high-end version of what depression is on the low end. Burnout is a psychological and physical state that requires a recovery cycle just to get back to normal.

Once you hit burnout, you cannot keep going. Just like when you fall into depression you need the recovery cycle to get back to normality of your natural zone of velocity.

An Edge Learner really is somebody who's found the edges of their natural state – not the upper or lower state. Their Zone of Natural Velocity. Edge Learners understand intimately their optimum state of velocity.

Back to the example of NASCAR. A car may have a maximum speed of 200 miles an hour. But the car can't sustain that speed all day long. It's got a cruising speed that it can sustain for hours and hours unless it runs out of fuel. We need to know our cruising speed - that's your optimum, natural velocity.

Of course, remember that slippery slope we talked about earlier. Society rewards high velocity more than low velocity. So, if society rewards higher velocity, shouldn't everybody want to be high velocity? No. Every person should understand their own natural velocity whether at lower, moderate or high.

What's also important to mention, that we need to understand is when you are in THE ZONE you are the best you can be for now. That doesn't mean you can't become better generally. But better is not going to be achieved by increasing your velocity. It'll be achieved by improving your skills and knowledge.

An Edge Learner rarely challenges their natural velocity. It doesn't matter whether they're high, medium or low, but they'll apply that natural velocity to get the most out of their capacity, without pushing so far as to end up in burnout or depression.

An Edge Learner has recognized how to monitor their symptoms. When they feel the nervousness and anxiety, they know they are pushing too much. They'll look for something to postpone, streamline, delegate or drop.

When thinking about an organization, a family, or a unit larger than an individual, many things that makeup that unit require only low velocity. Answering the phone, delivering the goods, taking an order, fulfilling the order, stocking the shelves, checking the quality, locking up at night, sending notes out to the people. All of those are low velocity things unless you try to do them simultaneously. Most of every day is low velocity work for everybody.

But if you're doing seven things at once, that adds up to high velocity even if all those are low velocity activities.

You can operate in a state of low velocity, but if you want to challenge yourself, take things up a notch, then you either need tools that take it off your shoulders, or people that allow you to delegate or farm it out, or systems and processes that make it easier for you to achieve more with less effort. Tools, systems and people resources allow people with low natural velocity to achieve high velocity things over time. High velocity people need those things to free them up to keep pushing the envelope.

Now in every organization, there are certain situations that are either a momentary crisis or a continuing recurring crisis, like hitting a sales deadline every month or whatever that crisis happens to be. The high velocity people are the ones that best address the urgency, marshaling all the resources wisely and being in control in the midst of the chaos. They say, "I work best under pressure." The lower velocity people quickly get overwhelmed by that. This is not a matter of intelligence - you could be absolutely Einstein-level brilliant yet with low velocity. It would not diminish your ability at all, it would simply diminish the pace for you.

Moderate velocity people are most of the people we know. (This is consistent with our research at the Carefree Institute while Jim was profiling thousands of business leaders in North America during the years 1988-92. Robert Kriegel's book The C Zone explores the same concept.) Mihaly Csikszentmihalyi in his book *Flow; the psychology of optimal experience*, described the same underlying concept, one's natural velocity or zone of optimal performance.

Probably 40% to 50% of people have a moderate zone of velocity. Worldwide natural velocities trend in that moderate zone. And in the higher zone, you've got maybe 10-15%. In the lower zone, 20%.

The challenge is that most folks need to let go of the idea that since high velocity is rewarded more, everyone should want to try to become high velocity.

Wrong. Not only wrong, but a damagingly bad idea for the individual! So that's why resources, relationships, tools, and systems are the way for any velocity of person to increase their capacity, and achievement.

You've heard the common saying, "Work smarter, not harder." It's easier said than done. I like to work both smart and hard, but I've found that efforts toward both can be wasted if there are no strategies and procedures in place.

WORK SMARTER NOT HARDER

1. Automate whatever repetitive tasks you can.
2. Delegate or outsource as many as possible of the tasks you can't automate.
3. Eliminate anything that's weighing you down or holding you back.
4. Then go to work on the item that matters most right now.

CHAPTER 8

MOTIVATION AND MILESTONES

If we could just figure out how to motivate people (in other words, figure out their drive) then we can get people to reach the desired outcomes we want.

Motivation and Drive is rooted in your Natural Values
But drive depends on 3 things:
1. How motivated you are
2. The clarity of your values
3. Your sense of connection with your goals

There are two kinds of motivation: extrinsic and intrinsic.

Extrinsic motivation occurs when we try from the outside to provide a motive for some action or behavior. Training a dog for example, requires stimulating extrinsic motivation for the dog: shake a paw and we give them a treat. The same might go for a sales team – the one with the most sales gets a financial bonus.

Intrinsic motivation occurs when we are moved to action because of our internal desire. My twin daughters both really want a phone. We've told them they can't have a phone until they have enough money to pay for the monthly fees of maintaining their phone.

They've decided to find ways to earn money to pay for the monthly fees of their phone. They are internally motivated to find a way to pay for the phone.

That's intrinsic motivation—when we make a conscious effort to achieve a goal because we want it, not because someone else sold us on it. The secret to great leadership is to find out what the intrinsic motivations of your followers are, then gear the extrinsic motivators to appeal to those.

Extrinsic: If I hold a gun to your head and tell you to stop procrastinating, do you think you'll be motivated to start taking action? Similarly, if I offer you a million dollars if you can stick to your exercise routine for just one more week, I'd predict you could accomplish that as well. By taking control of these associations and continuously reinforcing them, we can strengthen our motivation and drive to reach our desired goals.

Intrinsic motivation will make you want to jump out of bed each morning and it will keep you thinking about your goals until you go to bed. Motivation is one of the core components to drive.

The key to intrinsic motivation is in a person's value system, because values shape who you are and direct why you do what you do.

"When your values are clear to you, making decisions becomes easier." - Roy E. Disney

The Seven Natural Values

Natural values are part of who you are. Learned values are the ones you picked up from parents, school, friends, society, and church. Our focus here is on your Natural Values.

When you truly know what you really care about, not what mom and dad told you to care about, not what church or society tells you should care about, but what you honest to God really in your heart of hearts, soul of souls, really do care about – what you value – you will have figured out what motivates the drive in you.

Your values will give you a strong sense of what you truly want. Anyone can develop a burning passion and drive for their goals that excites the mind and makes us feel like we are truly living. Drive is a trait common to virtually any successful person in any field.

Each of us has a unique set of values. Values are what you care about; the qualities you find desirable.

They are the importance of something to you relative to your other options. Values are not attitudes, nor behaviors, though they form the basis of our attitudes and behaviors. Every decision we make is based on our own set of values.

Here is a value system model based loosely on the works of Edvard Spranger of the University of Berlin and the more contemporary work of Gordon Allport that Jim Cathcart calls the Natural Values Model.

In Jim's research he found seven values that are common to everyone. These aren't values we've learned, rather they're part of who we are.

These seven natural values are with you at birth and stay with you throughout your life. These values are in the acorn, the seed that is you, part of your very nature.

They are:

- Sensuality—the relative importance of one's physical experience
- Empathy—the relative importance of feeling connected to other people
- Wealth—the relative importance of ownership and tangible value

SEW

- Power—the relative importance of control and recognition
- Aesthetics—the relative importance of beauty, balance, order and symmetry
- Commitment—the relative importance of being committed to something, having a cause or mission, doing the "right" thing
- Knowledge—the relative importance of learning, discovering and understanding

PACK

SEW PACK

If you will picture a sewing kit with seven different colors of thread this will help you remember and understand this concept. Each thread is basically the same. Same fabric, same strength, same length, but different colors. Is any of the seven threads any better or more important than the others? No. They are the same except for color. So that means that some are suited to certain uses that the others would not go well with. The same is true for your values. None is nobler, better, more important than the others.

All are equal, except to you.

You and I have preferences, priorities. We feel more strongly about some values than others.

When I know your top values, I also know what motivates you. Your "motives" are rooted in what you feel is most important, your values.

If you value Knowledge most highly then you'll be motivated to learn. A book would be a good birthday gift to you. If your Knowledge value is low then a book would be a disappointing gift. You might look at the book and ask, "They didn't have chocolates?"

To understand the natural values better refer to Jim's bestselling book The Acorn Principle. ISBN 978-0-312-24284-8.

Micro-Milestones

Earlier, Jim briefly referenced micro-milestones: the act of breaking your goal down to the smallest possible fragment(s) to work on right away to start building momentum. As you continue to work and reward yourself, this momentum will build until it is almost unstoppable. Remember, you control your motivation.

As Lisa has identified, an Edge Learner has done the work to determine what are their values and recognizes how their values motivate their drive.

Recently, Lisa had a coaching session with here executive business coach, Barbara Reppert, about how you can't teach drive in others. What you can do is determine what their values are and then adapt your behavior to support those values to motivate them to activate their drive.

Do you remember the story of the tortoise and the hare? The hare ran very fast but got cocky and slacked off and lost the race. The tortoise moved very slowly, but consistently and won the race. The tortoise and the hare is an excellent metaphor for understanding the nature of our individual velocity.

Let's discuss drive in more detail. Once we determine drive, we can better understand velocity. Your velocity is the key to success.

Motivation is Motive in Action. Action is the intensity and energy and all the physical capacity. Motive is the drive.

As Zig Ziglar says, "Motivation follows action." Don't wait to be motivated to start acting. Start right now.

Your drive comes from clarifying what you care about and knowing what your value priorities are. So if the value for you is in power, the importance of control and recognition, whether your velocity is high, moderate or low doesn't matter. If you find it important to be in the VIP list, the person in charge, the one with a corner office, the one who gets to call the shots, if that's important to you, then me giving you special privileges is a big deal to you. I could be giving you cash, and it wouldn't nearly impress you as much as the corner office would.

Side note: Regardless if you're low or high, all of these things are separate from behavioral style.

Most of the world says, all of this boils down to behavioral style. This is where I disagree with the rest of the world. That would be like saying all of this boils down to one's skin. It's all the things under that skin that make that skin take the shape and do the things it's going to do.

Goal setting is vitally important to activating your drive.

You need to figure out *your* way of setting goals and clarifying your desired outcomes and keeping them in front of you in the appropriate ways for you.

Let's say you're our employee. If we can help you clarify what you care about, show you how our work relates to your values, then we are enlisting you emotionally, not just intellectually.

Then we'll help you set goals. We're specific as to the behaviors that will lead to the outcomes and cause the habits and become the systems that make all of this possible, because a system is to an organization what a habit is to a person. I'm a morning person, so my systems are to get out of bed early, wash my face, brush my teeth, put on my clothes, eat my breakfast, greet my day, right? That's a system. That's a habit that I put in place, but it's a system followed almost all the time.

Same thing on the job. Turn on the lights, unlock the door, turn on the outdoor signage so people know we're open, then log on to the computer, etc.

Systems are habits. Organization's systems (habits) are critical tools for individuals to achieve the things they want without having to think them up anew every single day.

So if every day you had to say, I want to preserve my teeth and not have bad breath. What should I do today? Well, yesterday you brushed your teeth. Yeah, but that was yesterday. Um, maybe I'll gargle I don't know, you know?

An Edge Learner really understands what drives and clarifies their priorities. What keeps them on target to achieve their goals or derails them. They know what their natural values are, not just their learned values. They understand their natural values, and it propels them, it keeps them on the edge of all those opportunities.

And the beauty of this is once we understand all this, we can go back and read it. We can examine our systems, our habits, and let our habits sort of audition to be adopted once again. So we can stop and have a moment of re-thinking to consider whether this system is serving us.

The Covid19 Lockdown: While writing much of this book, we were in quarantine. Now is the perfect opportunity to do some re-thinking. However, quarantine aside, the rule of thumb for re-thinking should be done every year.

You rethink by taking one part of your life at a time, whether that be your physical life, social life, business life, intellectual life, and examine it closely to see if you want to stay the course or change the course. That process is a big velocity boost. Once you're clear that you're headed toward what you want, in a way that is pretty much proven to work for you, dang, get out of the way!

Clarifying our drive and reminding ourselves of our goals by visualizing the outcomes stimulating those juices once again. That's how those things figure into keeping you at the top of your zone of velocity. But you also need to give yourself permission to vacillate up and down within that zone of velocity. Because if you're always at the upper edge, you're going to start going over the edge too often. And always at the lower edge, you're going to start dropping below it too often.

When you feel the dysfunction coming on, you need to interrupt your pattern.

This could mean, actually physically getting up from your desk and going for a walk. Interrupt the pattern. The pattern interruption creates the space for things to change. If you never interrupt the pattern, the pattern owns you.

If the way you motivate yourself to take action is by procrastinating until it's an emergency then you are not in control. That's not motivation. Procrastination is still dictating your actions until you no longer have a choice. At the point of urgency, the task enslaves you, you have to do it or fail. Procrastination leads to short term slavery.

Without pattern interruption, you can't create the space for opportunity. A new thought, new relationship, new opportunity, whatever that happens to be – innovation needs room to breathe.

Occasionally, we need to be a little bit overwhelmed. We need to be a little afraid. Not afraid for our lives, but afraid we might mess up.

Once Lisa was forced to make a pivot in her career and close a door to a business that she had breathed her soul into. When she rebounded, she had the second best year of her career up to that point. She kept her act together, learned from her previous experiences and entered back into the marketplace with clarity of her values, her purpose, highly motivated with an activated "prey drive," (a term coined by Coach Michael Burt) and a full force of velocity.

Organizations also have a natural velocity. The velocity in an organization comes more from the vision, mission, values and purpose at the core than it does from a person at the core.

Apple is a high velocity organization. Tesla, another high velocity organization. Uber, another. They've all emerged in short periods of time in revolutionary ways and had epic levels of demand placed upon them.

Now let's look at General Electric. GE has had moments in time over the years that acted in high velocity, but it has become a medium velocity organization. Why? Because it's an ongoing sustainable corporation that operates with high velocity over here for a while and then drops that off, normalizes it, outsources it or sells that division.

Governments tend to be low velocity. They are the lowest of the low velocity because they are sustained artificially by taxes. They don't have to keep themselves alive. They require our success in order to stay successful.

Life mostly works just fine if it's left to natural processes, but it's not necessarily kind because it is survival of the fittest. Those that don't choose to stay fit do fade away. High velocity companies typically have the most Edge Learners within them. Edge Learners in a government agency would make the government agency more efficient.

Recently a career opportunity was presented to me within an educational institution. I turned down the opportunity, not because the educational institution wasn't offering a great opportunity, or that I wasn't qualified for the position, but because I knew that I wasn't the right fit for the organization because we operate at different levels of velocity. I would be bothered by the limitations of an institution and probably more ambitious than them, thus creating conflict from the start.

Fishing is a great example of *apparent* low velocity. But the speed is not the deal, right? You can approach it like a nap and just relax into it, or you can make an obsession of it. I've got a friend who's absolutely a perfectionist in the highest and best sense of that word. His drive is high. His intensity though measured and methodical is also high. But if you observed him you would think he had low velocity.

He is dedicated to the point of almost insanity, and he loves fly fishing. He can tell you about every strand on every feather on every lure created and where it's placed in the water and why. He can tell you what the angle of the trout's mouth was when it took the lure. He knows beyond the need to know. But he's advancing the craft. And he loves it!

Commercial fishing on the high seas, on the other hand – high risk, high intensity, and therefore apparent high velocity. Flying an airplane, on the other hand? Not so much. It's hours of status quo punctuated by moments of deep intensity. But the routine-looking activity belies the intensity of focus required. It's people who have success velocity, not things.

TRY IT YOURSELF

Now look at your organization and ask: Are we generally a higher, moderate or lower velocity organization?

If we're a higher velocity organization, then we're going to require a greater percentage of high velocity people on our team. But in our support staff, we'll seek out moderate and lower velocity people.

Look at any sports organization – the Dallas Cowboys football team, for example. The players on the field are exceeding the limits that people thought were humanly possible and doing amazing entertaining moments that thrill the world. And those people get paid millions for being those players.

But those players also require locker rooms and buses and food and uniforms and everything that goes with being a sports organization. The coaches themselves don't have to necessarily be high velocity people. They have to be good strategists, systems people, good analysts, good researchers, good encouragers, supporters, nurturers, motivators; none of these roles are intrinsically high velocity, though they can be.

But the vast majority of the functions of any organization are low velocity. We need to have the right people in the right roles throughout the organization.

Once you feel at ease with this concept, you'll start to see the patterns in your own life, and subsequently, see the exceptions. You'll see times when you were on the high end and times you were at the low end, and how that drive and intensity ebb and flow. Once you embrace that, it's like embracing your intellectual bandwidth. Once you're totally comfortable with being as intelligent as you are, not more naturally intelligent than that, or as intense as you are and not more intense than that, then your life is in control. The stress goes out of your life because judgment goes away and you stop comparing yourself to others. The only person running this race is you.

CHAPTER 9

INCREASING INTENTIONALITY

The higher the percentage of intentionality in your work and your life, the more successful you will be.

Acting with intention is the key to everything! In our context, operating with intention means the answer to the question of "Why did you do that?" is always -- "because I meant to." You acted because the opportunity and your values were compatible so it made sense to do it.

When you're asked, how it was that something turned out so well, you'll answer, "Well, I had this idea. I did some research. I made a plan and stayed with it until it was finished. Of course, I had to adapt and adjust things along the way, but I stayed focused on the end game--my intention to succeed." That's an example of being intentional.

Intelligently curious people are creative. They're open to learning about and trying new things. They follow the directive from motivational speaker, Tony Robbins, to make C.A.N.I. their motto. It means to work for Constant And Never-ending Improvement. Unless you believe you've already attained a state of perfection, there are always ideas, strategies or plans that can be made for improvement. It just takes intention.

People who live intentionally are curious about everything. They love learning and want answers to all of life's questions. They constantly seek to expand their knowledge and try new things. It's been proven that those who are eager to learn are happier and more fulfilled than those who allow themselves to settle or stagnate in their development.

How Fully are You Living?

Being intentional requires planning and action. Intentionality makes sense for even the simplest things. We all practice it to some extent. The point of this chapter is to learn how to increase intentionality in everything. Stop living or conducting business on auto-pilot. While having systems in place is wise and helpful, don't allow yourself to become complacent with their use. Invest the time to analyze each of those systems every now and then to look for potential improvement. You wouldn't just get in your car and drive it everyday without occasionally taking it in to the mechanic for maintenance. It's important to consider potential maintenance needs in every aspect of your life.

The most common areas to evaluate are these:

1. Mental
2. Physical
3. Family
4. Social
5. Spiritual
6. Career
7. Financial
8. Emotional

Consider your percentage of intentionality in each of those categories.

When were you last intentional about your development in each of them?

Take each one and write down the % of intentionality you have been showing in that area lately. For example; if you have not intentionally read new blogs, books, articles, or listened to podcasts, books on tape, lectures, or watched informative videos outside of the entertainment on TV or online, then your percentage of intentionality would be low.

On the other hand, if you have a particular area of interest and have set up a routine of study, research and exploration in that category then your percentage would be higher. Increase your intentional actions.

What is your daily intention about the improvement of your mind? Do you go about your day without feeding your mind with something positive or interesting? Seek out a "go to" book that interests or inspires you and read from it daily or listen to it as you commute. Develop simple awareness practices, daily mind exercises; noticing the texture of your clothing or the variety of colors on your coffee mug or the various shapes of plants you see on your daily commute. Notice more than you need to. Being present enough to notice these things is calming to our minds.

What are your daily intentions about caring for your **body**? Fitness, relaxation, nutrition, and movement all are important. Make a plan, do each exercise on purpose.

How intentional are you--every day--about the quality of your relationships with family, friends and neighbors? The fallout from the COVID-19 pandemic has brought to the forefront the value of personal relationships to our mental health. Make a plan to spend at least a few minutes in intentional dialogue with someone daily.

Next is spiritual. The category of "spiritual" does not refer just to what you believe or whether you attend a church. Spirituality is the nurturing and living of your spirit. If you don't believe in or care about what you do, and feel that you're doing something noble, you won't do it nearly as well as if you did. Everyone has a spirit or soul. And everyone has a "religion", something they believe in, even if it is science or politics. Whatever your beliefs are rooted in is your "religion." But your spirit is independent of your beliefs. You believe with your mind. You have Faith with your soul. You must be doing something that brings you satisfaction, pride and dignity. Your spirit is where your "why" comes from. Without the "why," it's impossible to be intentional.

Your career intentionality is directly related to finding and creating opportunities. When Jim was just a "rosy-cheeked kid" he attended a Zig Ziglar seminar. He scraped together the $20 it took to buy one of Zig's books. He then swallowed his fear and stood in line to have the book autographed. When he decided to become a professional speaker himself, Jim set a goal to one day be the president of the National Speakers Association. His intention was to go from being the new kid on the circuit to earning the admiration and respect of those he looked up to. By increasing his 360-degree awareness for opportunities, creating and acting on his intentions, he achieved that position among others. In fact, he ended up becoming friends with Zig and doing work with and for the Ziglar Corporation and becoming considered one of the Ziglar Learning "family members."

When it comes to intentionality with regard to money, the time to learn how to manage it is when you don't have any. Remember the story about Jim's son learning how to manage money when he received his first allowance? If you only have a small amount you need to be darn careful with every penny. When you have larger sums, you'll be able to absorb a potential loss on a more risky or challenging venture. You should know where your money comes from and where it goes daily.

Few things motivate people more than debt. Yet it is a negative energy. If you look at some of the most successful people today, they often have similar stories: They came from hardship. They had nothing. They struggled to make ends meet. One such example is Oprah Winfrey. She came from nothing and became one of the richest women on the planet! Getting out of debt isn't done by a big lottery win, it is done day to day through wise financial decisions.

When Lisa was trying to start her own private investigation firm in Edmonton, it was a make or break time for her. If she could not get it off the ground, she would have to move back to Saskatchewan and live at home. She had not lived at home since she was 17 years old and couldn't imagine moving home after six years of living on her own. She delivered close to 100 portfolio documents for the PI firm, made cold calls to every law firm and insurance firm in Edmonton and knocked on as many doors. Also during this time, she was sending out resumes for 'real jobs' and even went on an interview with a bank and was hired. The day she accepted the bank job, she also received her first contract to complete a PI job for an insurance company with a budget of $1200. The bank job was abandoned and the rest, as they say, was history.

The next aspect of your life in which to be intentional is emotional. This is a big one. Depending on where you look, between 25 and 30 human emotions have been identified. These include: Fear, Anger, Sadness, Joy, Surprise, Anticipation, Grief, Love, Admiration and Boredom. We believe it's important to evaluate how many emotions we are allowing to express themselves through us and how do we handle those emotions?

If a dear friend dies, do you allow myself to grieve? Or do you deny your feelings and push on as if it didn't happen? The reality is that grief must be addressed. The longer we put it aside or delay it, the more intense it will be. Rather than having a brief period of depression, we may end up with a physical illness or require therapy to work through that grief. It's been proven that some severe physical illnesses are the manifestation of unmet emotional needs. Intentionally allowing ourselves to experience and deal with both the positive and negative emotions that are part of life is critical to our overall emotional health.

All emotions have their own cycles not unlike what happens to the physical body. When we have a broken bone or skinned knee, we don't deny it happened and push on. Our body has processes it must go through to get back to a healed state. It works the same way with the heart, the spirit and the mind. When we take an emotional hit, we go through the identifiable stages of grief: Denial, Anger, Bargaining, Depression and Acceptance. Let your emotions happen but manage how you express them.

It's important to respect our emotions and realize our minds cannot control our emotions. We can only observe and accommodate them. We can compartmentalize our emotions for a time but eventually, it's best to deal with them--whether negative or positive. Sometimes having a good old belly laugh or even laughing until we cry is so important. It's because when that happens, we're feeling our emotions on a deep level.

A friend asked Jim for advice. The friend was quite successful by most standards but wasn't excited about life anymore. "He invited me to his house for a visit and offered to pick me up. He showed up in a Rolls Royce! We drove into his circular drive with its 40-foot tall Christmas tree (brought to Florida from the State of Washington). We entered his mansion and he gave me a tour of the home and grounds: tennis court, pool, exercise room--all the amenities most people dream of. Yet, he wasn't happy."

He said, "Jim, every goal I set, I absolutely know I will achieve it. I've got everything a person could want. I have a good marriage, a good life. I'm financially secure. Yet I'm still not happy."

Jim said, "I wasn't sure why he was asking *me* for advice and told him so."

He said, "Now, come on, Jim. You've got an essence about you that I want in me. It's not about how much money you have. It's just that you've got a sense of inner peace and at the same time, excitement about living that I want to recapture in me."

Jim thought about that for a moment and said, "It all comes from my *reason* for doing what I do. It's not about *the doing*. It's about what I get from doing what I do."

Jim then asked him what he cared most about, what fueled that inner emotion, his drive to make a difference in the world. They talked about what would scare him if he didn't achieve it. Jim helped him to remember how it felt when he first started his path to success and to think about what would make him feel that way again. He helped him focus on increasing his intentionality.

The M.O. Grid: Mode of Operation (Modus Operandi)

When it comes to increasing intentionality there are basically two dimensions.

1. Thinking
2. Doing

Thinking involves awareness and a sense of knowing. Doing involves behavior and performance. Each area is weighed on a scale with low at the bottom left and high at the top right. This grid creates four modes of operation. Four quadrants are: Low Awareness/Low Performance, Low Awareness/High Performance, High Awareness/Low Performance and High Awareness/High Performance. "Low/Low, Low/High, High/Low, High/High."

Passenger Mode

Those with low intentionality are also likely to have low awareness and performance. When you don't know much, you don't do much. This could also be identified as the "passenger" mode. They want to get to a certain destination but don't want or need the responsibility of getting there. To increase their intentionality, these folks also need to increase either their knowledge or their performance.

Critic Mode

People who have high awareness but under-perform (low performance) are often seen as being "Critics." They *know* what to do but choose not to do much of it. Improving intentionality for them is simply a matter of acting on their knowledge.

Competitor Mode

There are those high performers with low awareness. These people are seen as being "Competitors." They take a lot of action but don't invest time in thinking much about those actions. Not all activities need a competitive approach. To increase their intentionality, they would benefit from periodic analysis of their actions to ensure they're doing the right things--being intentional about the actions that will improve the results they're getting.

Leader Mode

Leaders have both high awareness and they perform at a high level. They know a lot (and continue to learn a lot). They think about their actions and do more than is required of them. To reach their highest levels of achievement, these people only need to build solid support systems around themselves.

When you work on increasing intentionality, you'll likely be in each mode at some time or another. Each has a time and place. When others are in charge of a situation and you don't have a reason to act, you'll likely be in passenger mode. Examples of this are when you are literally a passenger or when you've taken on something new. As a passenger, it's time to sit, observe, listen and learn.

There will be times when it's important to settle into critic mode--to research and analyze your next best course of action. You may test out different strategies and approaches or even involve others in taking action on your behalf.

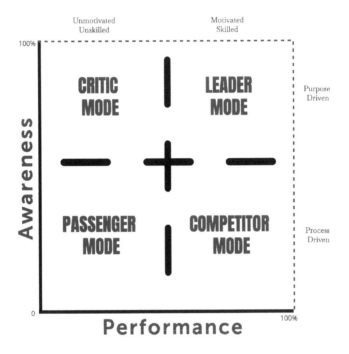

TRY IT YOURSELF

When it's time to act intentionally, it's time to be proactive. This is when you put on your competitor armor and dive into the fray yourself--taking those actions you've decided are best at that time and place.

The most productive mode when considering increasing intentionality is the leader mode. This is when you will be most proactive. This is when it'll be time for you to take action and make things happen. Ask yourself, which mode have I been in the most lately in each main area of my life?

If you discover that you are low on the "thinking" scale, it's time to increase your education. Notice more, learn more, know more.

If you are low on the "doing" scale, where you feel your performance is too low, it's time to re-think your motivation. But more than that, it is time to take action. Do something! Even if it is a small positive action, TAKE ACTION.

Whatever you do, do it because that is what you meant to do.

Be More Intentional!

CHAPTER 10

WHAT ARE YOUR PSYCHOLOGICAL BLIND SPOTS?

"Honestly officer, I didn't even see the other car. I never would have proceeded if I had seen him!" Many traffic cops have heard that statement.

Everyone has blind spots. It is physically provable. A portion of each eye has a place in the retina that does not perceive images. But our minds, ever our protectors, have devised a solution. They simply cause us to not notice our microscopic blindness. It's true, we don't even notice that we aren't seeing some things.

Psychological Blind Spots

Likewise we each have psychological blind spots. These are the result of how we think and what we believe or care about. If we love puppies then we can look at a public park and instantly notice the puppies. Those who don't particularly care about dogs can look at the same exact scene and not notice them. But they'll "see" things that we don't.

For example, if you believe that the world is plagued with racism then you will tend to interpret statements others make as if they had racial implications. If you are trained as a pilot then you will habitually notice weather, visibility, and other aviation factors that most overlook. If you are a painter, the first thing you see is the way the item is painted, then you see the item. Designers see the fashion and maybe not the person wearing it.

That's why Lisa Patrick is such an ideal coauthor for this book. She has been trained as a private investigator to constantly see what other people miss. When she and Jim interviewed researchers, law enforcement officers and investigators, they found the same skill of "Edge Learning" to be present in all of them. They weren't just curious, they were intelligent about their curiosity. You can acquire this skill too.

Physical Blind Spots

Here's an exercise that can reveal where your blind spots are in each eye.

X   O

On a sheet of white paper draw an X on the left and an O on the right, about six inches apart, near the center of the paper. Make them large enough to easily see but small enough to disclose your blind spot, about one inch high. The size of a man's thumbnail.

With the paper in your right hand, close your left eye. Focus your attention on the X and only the X. Notice whether you can still see the O without changing your point of focus. If the O is still visible, slowly move the paper toward your face with your attention only on the X. (If you look at the O, of course, you will always see it.)

At some point in this process the O will fall into your blind spot. It's there, but you won't see it in peripheral vision. That's your blind spot. Now, close your right eye and focus your left eye only on the O. Change the paper to your left hand.

Looking only at the O, repeat the exercise and notice when the X drops into your blind spot. Most people can do this after a few tries. If you find this difficult, the key is to focus only on the target letter and not look for the other letter. It doesn't fall into a black hole. What happens instead is, the O or X is positioned in your blind spot and your mind simply fills in the gap to look like its surroundings and you don't notice the gap.

If this is true physically, how much more true is it for our psychological blindspots?

Let's go back to the traffic officer interviewing the driver who caused an accident. Assume that you are the officer. Your natural curiosity will cause you to ask questions and examine the scene, but your psychological blindspots may obscure the truth.

For example; if you have a strong bias toward people of a certain type, you will assume they have good intentions. If your bias is against that type of person, then you may assume they have bad intentions or were negligent. Your questions might be the same with each person but the way you "hear" their answer would vary based on your preferences, biases, or judgments of the source.

In a courtroom, much time is spent interviewing potential jurors to determine their biases and potential blindspots. As facts and evidence are presented, all jurors hear and see the same information, but they react differently.

Everyone is blind to some things. We cannot avoid it, we only see those things that lie in the general direction that we are looking. The same is true of points of view attitudinally. If you feel strongly about something then its opposite will not automatically become noticeable. As philosopher Kevin Buck says, "Without reflection there is no true learning."

Check yourself on the following statements and note how many of them you feel are true. Then take some time to reflect on what blindspots might occur from holding only one point of view.

- Big business is a potential threat, we need regulations and oversight to keep them from exploiting people and resources.
- Government is our friend. We can trust them when we can't trust others.
- Government is the least effective manager and should be limited to only a minimum of functions.
- Police officers are good people who bravely watch out for the rest of us.
- Police officers are potentially dangerous to honest citizens, they need restraints on their power.
- Successful people have earned their rewards. They already pay more in taxes than average citizens and should not be taxed more than others.
- Successful people should be obligated to share their wealth with others.
- People are generally good and most of them can be trusted.
- People are potentially dangerous and greedy. We need protection from others.
- Education is a personal responsibility.
- Education is a public responsibility.
- Medicine and doctors are angels.
- Medicine and doctors are threats.

- Life is what you make of it. Success is possible for anyone.
- Life is a matter of luck. Some people never get a break.
- Life has a purpose.
- Life is just that, life. It has no higher purpose.
- Dogs are dangerous, basically they are wolves that have been tamed.
- Dogs are "man's best friend", they make life more joyful.
- Motorcycles are "murder cycles", people die from riding them.
- Motorcycles are "freedom machines", they allow you to see the world in wonderful new ways.
- Guns are tools of death and should be eliminated or limited to soldiers and law officers.
- Guns are protective devices and everyone should be able to defend themselves.

Your authors don't care what your answers were to these questions, but you do. Our goal was simply to expose you to some judgmental points of view that might reveal your blindspots. All of the above perspectives have an opposite that is undesirable to those who embrace these views. All of them.

The stronger you feel about an issue, the more likely you are to have a psychological blind spot when looking at data or people connected to that.

There is no score to be derived from your answers here because there was no test. This is a list of points of view designed to stimulate reflection and introspection. The first step in eliminating your blindspots is to become aware that they exist.

How does it affect your actions?

The next step is to examine how they appear in your performance day to day.

Who do you always listen to? Who do you feel has nothing valuable to say?

What subjects cause your mind to slam shut to further information?

In a recent conversation with close friends we started discussing political personalities. The instant the name Trump came up, all further discussion was rejected as biased. Wow! It was as if one who agreed with anything related to Trump was suddenly rejected on all topics and views. "No value can be gained on any level from one who might not hate Trump." That is an amazingly close-minded view. This is an example of eagerly embraced blind spots. The person just summarily rejected anything that was favorable to Trump or his point of view.

Do you have some hot-button issues or persons who just make your mind shut out further information? Most people do. Getting beyond our biases takes practice, intent and training.

Remember, you only know what you know until someone else gives you new information or another way of looking at things. If your curiosity can be shut down with biases then you cannot achieve Intelligent Curiosity.

Listening to an opponent doesn't require endorsing them or approving of them. It just means that you will acquire their information in addition to your own.

Know Thyself: use the models in this book to explore your personal values, your natural velocity, your behavioral style and how you are regarded by others.

The better you know yourself, the less you will judge yourself
The less you judge yourself, the more you will accept yourself
The more you accept yourself, the more you will accept others
The more you accept others, the less you will judge them
The less you judge them, the more you will cooperate with them
The more we cooperate, the better we will make the world for everyone.

Intelligent Curiosity

This entire book has been about reflection on what matters and how to discover more. Our goal has always been to shift your perspective to the edges and show you what to become curious about. The payoff of this new Edge Learning skill of Intelligent Curiosity is discovery and understanding. You will become progressively more aware and better informed.

TO KNOW MORE

Remember:

To KNOW more, NOTICE more

The more you NOTICE, the more you KNOW

The more you KNOW, the more OPTIONS you will see

The person who has the most OPTIONS and takes action creates opportunity and usually WINS.

Now what should you be wondering about? Where do you need to focus your attention to discover more?

BOOK SUMMARY

Chapter 1 - What is Intelligent Curiosity?

Intelligent curiosity is more than being generally interested in something. It is when you consciously choose to notice more than what is presented on the surface. You don't just notice something. You notice everything around it that impacts its existence.

Chapter 2 - Becoming an Eligible Receiver

Learn how to become open to attracting the results you desire. Develop the qualities that would cause others to want to do business with you. Be a magnet not just an arrow.

Chapter 3 - Where's The Problem?

A problem cannot be solved until it is identified. Questions to ask include: Who "owns" this problem? What is the cause, or source of the problem? Is it a Situational, Personal, Interpersonal, Technical or System problem? Make decisions using the Yes Or No model. Make a Personal Decision and a Practical Decision, then choose your best path.

Chapter 4 - Different Types of People are Curious Differently

There are many ways of being curious but people have patterns of curiosity that can be observed and understood. Once you know someone's pattern of personality, then you can predict what they will want to know first and how they will go about finding it. Assure that you can adapt your instinctive pattern to those around you.

Chapter 5 - Edge Learning

Don't just look at the painting, notice the frame and the wall where it hangs. Discover ways to draw people in with your wisdom by helping them stretch their own thinking, their own awareness. Edge Learning is not about memorizing facts, but rather developing those soft skills through real-world experiences and mentoring from leading experts and entrepreneurs.

Chapter 6 - Seeking 360-Degree Opportunities

Most people walk by opportunities every single day. Edge Learners understand this and are constantly on the lookout for what others miss. Developing a 360-degree awareness for opportunities is a learnable skill. This chapter will help the reader become aware of what others miss in the periphery.

Chapter 7 - Success Velocity

The rate of advancement toward a goal is "velocity." Everyone has a natural zone of velocity, either high, moderate or low. As long as they can stay within their natural zone then they can be at their best. Outside of your zone, you lose effectiveness rapidly.

Chapter 8 - Motivation and Milestones

Drive is rooted in one's Natural Values. When we know what they care about most, we also know how to motivate them, including ourselves. By establishing milestones, goals, to guide us, we can stay the course toward our desired outcomes. The Zone of Velocity is more important than the actions in a given moment when it comes to reading people's Optimum Velocity.

Chapter 9 - Increasing Intentionality

The greater the percentage of your day that is intentional, the greater your success will be. Don't just ask questions, have a plan and a system for doing so. High achievers have developed the skill of being highly intentional in every aspect of their daily lives from their sleeping patterns, to their morning routines, to how they dress, act and think. Recognize the value of becoming intentional in your own life and see examples of how those who are intelligently curious live their lives.

Chapter 10 - Where are Your Psychological Blind Spots?

Consider that everything you know has had to pass through the filter of your time available to learn it, the limits of your learning ability, the biases of those from whom you learned, the number of sources you explored, and the amount of testing you could do of each idea in actual practice. A 20 year old genius couldn't possibly know as much as a 60 year old average IQ person. They might know more on some topics, but overall they would know less. As Ralph Waldo Emerson said, "Every person is, in some ways, my superior. In that, I can learn from him." Know where you might most likely miss something important.

ABOUT THE AUTHORS

Jim Cathcart, CSP, CPAE

For four years in a row Jim Cathcart has been selected as one of the Top 5 Speakers on Sales & Service in an online survey of over 27,000 people. His TEDx video "How to Believe in Yourself" is in the Top 1% of all TED videos worldwide with over 2.4 million views. With over 44 years of professional speaking around the world, Jim Cathcart is one of the best known and most award-winning motivational speakers in the business. He has delivered more than 3,300 presentations to audiences in every state of the US, most provinces of Canada, 23 major cities in China, and countries from Scotland to Singapore. Some of his most recent international engagements were for thousands of business leaders in Bogota', Colombia; Costa Rica; Panama; Warsaw, Poland; Santiago, Chile and Penang, Malaysia!

He's a university professor in the Executive MBA program and Entrepreneur in Residence for the School of Management at California Lutheran University. He's a Certified Virtual Presenter. He calls himself "Your Virtual VP". From a business base in Austin, Texas he is a mentor, business strategist, psychological researcher and philosopher at heart, Jim is also a down to earth regular guy. He has worked in warehouses, driven trucks, sold donuts door to door, been a bank teller, plays guitar in night clubs and pubs, and has toured much of the world on a motorcycle.

Someone recently said, "Jim Cathcart is what 'Fonzie' would have been if he'd gone to business school." Fonzie was a character, a rebel, "the cool guy" in the TV series Happy Days. Jim was an insurance agent for many years, an Army officer and a bill collector who, while in his twenties, had to repossess log trucks in the mountains of northern Arkansas. From this varied background he decided in 1972 to become an authority on the subject of motivation and through decades of dedication, study and hard work, he made it happen.

Jim has been hired by the top corporations in the world in most industries and professions.

After hearing Earl Nightingale on the radio one day in 1972, Jim was inspired to change his life. While working as a government clerk in the Housing Authority, he became determined to learn psychology and master the process of self-improvement. Through years of fanatical dedication to this quest he learned new skills, became a certified trainer for a variety of programs, read stacks of books, attended countless seminars and volunteered thousands of hours to civic organizations. In this process he moved from clerk, to manager, to sales person, to leader, to trainer, to author and professional speaker.

Today he is listed in the Top Sales World Magazine Hall of Fame, the professional Speaker Hall of Fame, is a recipient of the prestigious Golden Gavel Award (along with Earl Nightingale, Art Linkletter, Walter Cronkite, Zig Ziglar and many others), has been the president of the National Speakers Association and received the Cavett Award for a lifetime of service. He has authored 21 books and scores of recorded programs. In 2020 he was listed as one of The Top 50 Keynote Speakers by Top Sales World magazine. The San Diego chapter of the National Speakers Association renamed their member of the year award "The Jim Cathcart Service Award" and the Greater Los Angeles chapter gave Jim the Lifetime Achievement Award in 2003. In 2008 he was inducted as one of the "Legends of the Speaking Profession."

Jim's 3,000+ client list includes most of the Fortune 500 plus: ASAE, ATRA, Motorola, Mass Mutual, Prudential, Norwest Bank, Becton Dickinson, John Deere, Levi Strauss, Ford, Mercedes Benz, BMW, American Airlines and the United States Air Force.

You can contact Jim at info@cathcart.com and through his many social media listings.

Cathcart website: https://cathcart.com
https://en.wikipedia.org/wiki/Jim_Cathcart
https://www.facebook.com/jim.cathcart
https://www.instagram.com/jimcathcart/
https://www.linkedin.com/in/cathcartinstitute/
https://www.youtube.com/channel/UCgjvZ_hNCmNcXG_i8H9BCyQ
https://vimeo.com/jimcathcart.
TEDx: https://youtu.be/-ki9-oaPwHs

Lisa Patrick

Integrator. Powerhouse Connector. Pit Bull. Queen of Persistence. Angelic Creator. Fearlessly Forward. Catalyst, Distinctively Unforgettable. These are just some of the word's clients have used to describe Lisa Patrick. A Silver Medal Podcast Finalist at Top Sales World, recently nominated for 2021 Women of Inspiration | Universal Women's Network, and the 2021 One-To-Watch, RBC Canadian Women Entrepreneur Award. A regular contributor at Forbes and Entrepreneur Magazine, an investor and managing partner at Belongify, and partner and master distributor at Assessments24x7 Canada.

Lisa is also the CEO of her own personal brand, speaking and consulting with other founders and busy executives who are looking for clarity and a proven methodology to take their ideas and knowledge to market and scale in an effort for founders to stay relevant and distinctive in an ever-changing market.

Lisa learned the art of entrepreneurship at an early age as the daughter of a retired RCMP officer, who grew up as an only child to two amazing parents on a grain farm in small-town Canada. Her experiences there set the foundation for the future development of Edge Learning skills.

Lisa's dad taught her how to be adaptable when necessary and execute with extraordinary commitment and drive. Her mom taught her it was ok to live in fear but to be fearless in her convictions. Most importantly, Lisa learned to value relationships above everything else and that sometimes the best option is not always the right one for everyone involved.

Growing up, Lisa was determined to become a police officer, she was that kid that only ever wanted to become a cop. Driven to the opportunity in an era largely dominated by men, Lisa was accepted as only 1 of 5 women to Grant MacEwan College in their Law Enforcement program. After graduating from Law Enforcement, Lisa worked in the Sex Crimes division in the City of Edmonton Police department. In this position, she quickly discovered that this was not where she wanted to be for the long term. Having enrolled in University, Lisa took a part-time job as a private investigator and was hooked! Ten credits shy of her degree, Lisa quit university and her part time position and started her own private investigation agency. During her time growing this successful agency, she maximized the skills necessary to read people, to be hyper-aware of her surroundings and to create opportunities to create successful outcomes.

Always on the lookout for new opportunities, she later moved onto a business that developed an online bookkeeping platform and software, which led to even greater opportunities. Lisa then launched XTRAcredits to provide accreditation services to authors, coaches, experts and thought leaders.

Lisa hosted her own podcast called "Coffee with Lisa," silver medal finalist for top sales and marketing podcast for 2020 at Top Sales World. Her guests are an eclectic group of world-renowned authorities, who share their stories and experiences in business and life over a cup of coffee. Guests include sales disruptor Lisa Copeland, Market Inventor, the godfather of Market Invention Adam Vasquez, several Hall of Fame professional speakers including war veteran Charlie Munger, NFL retired running back and former ESPN correspondent Merril Hoge, Professor Michael Solomon amongst others.

Lisa and her Belongify.com business partner, a retired Chief People Officer, considered the go-to interrupter for culture, Lorne Rubis started a podcast, Culture Uncorked; showcasing professionals from the C-suite, sharing stories and real-life experiences, proven techniques and challenges faced today in building extraordinary cultures. Guests have included: Garry Ridge, Chairman and CEO of WD40, retired CEO at Alberta Treasury Branch, Dave Mowat and current Chairman of the Board for Alberta Treasury Branch and Edmonton International Airport Joan Hertz, amongst others.

Today, you can find Lisa on and off stages driven by helping others create connection and discover opportunity. Lisa is also currently writing her second book.

You can contact Lisa at info@LisaPatrick.ca
and through her many social media channels.

Linkedin.com/in/clisapatrick
Facebook.com/lisapatrickbfd
Instagram.com/Lisapatrickbfd
JoinClubhouse.com/LisaPatrick
youtube.com/channel/UC6j2MDHXWIL_3jVLWv9NsTA

Connect   Meet Lisa

Jim Cathcart

Relationship Intelligence® Advanced Certification Program

Discover the expertise enterprises have been leveraging for years, now in a virtual, interactive setting. Jim will guide you through his 12-week master class designed for enterprises, entrepreneurs and sellers at all levels

cathcart.mentored.com

Turn Your Connections Into Assets!

What to Expect

Module 1: Profitable Business Friendships
Module 2: Reputation Management
Module 3: Sales Metrics
Module 4: The 8 Sales Competencies
Module 5: Up-Serving
Module 6: Create a Sales Culture
Module 7: Face To Face Selling
Module 8: The Changing Way People Buy
Module 9: Sales Negotiation
Module 10: Reading People
Module 11: Selling in Fast Times
Module 12: The Sales Mindset

 Live Webinars

 Expert Content

 Microlearning

 Quizzes & Assessments

 Mobile Responsive

Progress Tracking & Analytics

A virtual training experience focused on individual results and team ROI. 1:1 opportunities available.

mentored

lp. LISA PATRICK

building YOUR brand

GET STARTED
info@LisaPatrick.ca Today!

SUCCESSFULLY

From IDEAtion to BUILDout to SCALE!

lp. LISA PATRICK

Meet Lisa

development

SOCIAL MEDIA

FOLLOW LISA

Get Your Deck

GET DISC

Listen on Apple Podcasts

Listen Now

Join Me

BELONG

BE INTELLIGENTLY CURIOUS

Join Us